THE SON IN THE BIBLE AND THE CHURCH

Also by John Thurmer

A DETECTION OF THE TRINITY

THE SON
IN THE
BIBLE AND
THE CHURCH

John Thurmer

Chancellor of Exeter Cathedral

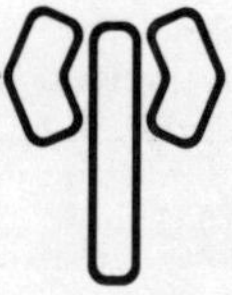

EXETER
THE PATERNOSTER PRESS

AUSTRALIA:
Bookhouse Australia Ltd.,
P.O. Box 115, Flemington Markets, NSW 2129

SOUTH AFRICA:
Oxford University Press,
P.O. Box 1141, Cape Town

British Library Cataloguing in Publication Data

Thurmer, John
   The son in the Bible and the church.
   1. Jesus Christ
   I. Title
   232   BT202

   ISBN 0–85364–449–7

Photoset in Great Britain by
Photoprint, 9–11 Alexandra Lane, Torquay, Devon
and printed for The Paternoster Press,
Paternoster House, 3 Mount Radford Crescent, Exeter, Devon
by A. Wheaton & Co. Ltd., Exeter.

Contents

Preface

All human language about the being of God is inadequate, and there is a proper silence in the presence of him with whom we have to do. But once we talk or write about God (as we must if we believe in him) then language had better do what it can, without invoking humility or mystery when it gets into difficulties. I take the need for humility and the fact of mystery as governing everything I write, and therefore make no particular mention of them in the course of the argument.

The 'languages' in the sense of the areas of study in this book are complex—the Bible, Christian doctrine, psychology. A reader may well think I am but modestly equipped to be trespassing so widely. But I am a working clergyman, trying to explain these things to myself and to others. A book like this is a by-product of half a century of praying, thinking and speaking (both public preaching and private counselling); it is, with explanation, 'how I see it'. And if, in the body of it, I do not write 'I think' or 'I feel' (or even 'A funny thing happened to me on my way to the publishers'), that is not because it does not arise from my experience. It is because at school they taught me not to use the first person singular in essays, and I am too set in my ways to change now.

I am grateful to my colleagues the Dean and Chapter of Exeter Cathedral for giving me a chance to put these thoughts together, and for a grant from the Bishop Phillpotts Trust to spend some time at that hospitable Gladstone shrine St. Deiniol's Library. It has been a comfort to work under the patronage of Henry Phillpotts and William Ewart Gladstone, those Victorian giants whose faith and works put our own puny efforts into perspective!

Introduction

From the fourth to the eighteenth century Christendom believed that Jesus of Nazareth was God the Son, the second person of the Holy Trinity. The church believed this, and the church believed that Jesus believed it as the basis of his life and self-consciousness. The Jesus of history and the Christ of faith were identical.

Since the rise of biblical and historical criticism two hundred years ago, the main-stream Christian churches have continued to subscribe to the belief of Christendom. But the western churches at least are less confident that their members are personally and individually committed to it; and scholars in the critical tradition often doubt, with due publicity, the official formulation of the belief. Even more, they doubt that Jesus believed anything like what the church subsequently claimed for him. Often, indeed, they fiercely deny that Jesus could, or did, believe any such thing.

The point is strongly made in the volume with the provocative title, *The Myth of God Incarnate*.[1] Michael Goulder tells an autobiographical anecdote against himself. In a hospital waiting room he was discussing Jesus with a Congregationalist minister who said, 'Well, one thing is certain; he didn't think he was the Second Person of the Trinity.' The remark led the writer from conceited anglican orthodoxy (his own self-evaluation) to liberalism and subsequently to unbelief.

1. Edited by John Hick, SCM 1977, pp. 48–9.

There *may* be no absolute conflict or contradiction between the truth (that Jesus is God the Son) and his own ignorance of the fact in his earthly life. This is one of the things that doctrines of *kenosis* (self-emptying) seek to accommodate. An impressive recent work, *The Divine Trinity*[2] restates the claim that there is no necessary contradiction between Jesus being God the Son and not knowing it.

But there is, to the plain man, something rather suspicious and discreditable about such an argument. It carries more than a hint of 'knowing better than Jesus about Jesus'. And satisfying the mind and conscience of the plain man ought to be one of the aims of Christian theology and one of the standards by which it is judged. The God who 'so loved the world' (John 3:16) and 'revealed these things to babes' (Matthew 11:25) *cannot* intend the truth about himself to be available only to scholars.

In a sense this book's starting point is the remark which Michael Goulder records. Its aim is to show that Jesus *did* think of himself as the second person of the Trinity. But this is not to ignore or dismiss the critical scholarship of the last two hundred years. The terminology of the 'Nicene' and 'Athanasian' creeds was not available to Jesus, and the word 'Trinity' does not appear in the New Testament. Could Jesus have known the core and essence of the trinitarian scheme without its later terminology? Or, to put it another way, can we re-unite the Jesus of history with the Christ of faith without abandoning the insights of criticism? I believe the answer to both questions is yes.[3]

The questions of church order and morality which occupy the later chapters are not exhaustive or free-standing treatments of their subjects, but attempts to relate the biblical and doctrinal understanding of sonship

2. David Brown, Duckworth 1985.
3. 'What is needed is a new vision of the biblical text which does justice not only to the demands of a thoroughly post-Enlighten-ment age, but also to the confessional stance of the Christian faith for which the sacred scriptures provide a true and faithful vehicle for understanding the will of God'—Brevard S. Childs, *The New Testament as Canon: An Introduction*, SCM 1984, p. 37.

to some of the things which loom large in the modern church. Church order and morals are not self-contained systems. They stem from belief, which in turn becomes incarnate in activity; as St. Paul, after eleven chapters of doctrine in the Epistle to the Romans, says, 'Therefore . . .' (Romans 12:1) and proceeds to give practical counsel. Church order and liturgy are living 'icons'[4] of what we believe; they are determined by belief and in turn help to mould it.

I have in mind, then, readers with some knowledge of modern thought who wish to maintain and strengthen their faith but are disappointed or alarmed, as I am, by much of what is now said and done. If this book comes into the hands of any who are unaffected by the critical tradition and entirely satisfied with the doctrine of the main-stream churches, I hope they can treat it as a meditation on that doctrine with some thoughts they may be able to make their own. Orthodoxy, however firm, must never be simply static. It must be personally and individually appropriated in thought and life. If it is not, it deserves the scourge of unbelief, as Christendom once deserved the scourge of the Hun and the Turk.

4. The Greek word *eikōn* means, simply, image. It is not limited to the particular sort of image found in an Eastern Orthodox church.

CHAPTER ONE

Beware of Titles

The official forms in which the modern world abounds require us to describe ourselves as 'Mr., Mrs., Miss or Title'. Getting titles right can produce a good deal of anguish and annoyance—from the ecclesiastic finding himself treated as a piece of artillery to the scholarly American who discovers that the Marquis of Blandford is a commoner. Theories of egalitarianism propounded by political revolutions may suppress one form of title but they soon create others. Titles are in fact a large part of the way human beings seek to understand and define themselves in relation to their fellows. We succeed to, or are appointed or elected to hold, certain titles. The forceful may create new titles for themselves and others.

A large part of the study of the New Testament is a matter of titles—whether Jesus claimed them or others applied them to him, and with what meaning or intention. A title, moreover, is not the same as a description, though some titles are also descriptive. To take an example from the ecclesiastical history of England: the Queen is sometimes referred to as head, or supreme governor, of the Church of England, and the impression is often given that this is a royal title. But it is not. Henry VIII awarded himself the title 'Head of the Church' in the course of his ecclesiastical revolution, and it was inherited by his son Edward VI and his daughter Mary I. But Mary disapproved of it and by due constitutional process removed it. Elizabeth I did not revive the title, though she revived most of the powers which accompanied it. It might, therefore, be thought to describe the relation of church to crown under the Elizabethan settlement; but it could not be used to deduce powers or procedures not defined elsewhere.

Who did Jesus think he was? Or who did the New Testament writers think he was? The possibility, to say the least, that there is some distinction between the two questions cannot be overlooked. A book is not the same thing as a person and a biography, however great, is not identical with its subject. Inspiration and authority may make the book (or books) uniquely precious. But they are books still, subject to everything that happens to books in this world. They are practically all we have, apart from the tradition of the church, to answer the question, Who did Jesus think he was?

The efforts of the first hundred years of critical study are described in Albert Schweitzer's *The Quest of the Historical Jesus.*[1] Readers of this famous and fascinating book are often amazed to discover how many 'modern' ideas about Jesus and the New Testament were in fact propounded a hundred, a hundred and fifty, or two hundred years ago. Most of the possible answers to the question, 'Who did Jesus think he was?' are in its course both asserted and denied—teacher of righteousness, prophet of the End, servant, messiah, Son of David, Son of Man, Son of God, man of destiny, freedom-fighter: the list is not exhaustive and they are not all mutually exclusive. But something controlled his self-understanding, and the church's understanding of him. Such power stems from clarity and unity of mind and purpose. In human terms, Jesus of Nazareth must have been a man of extraordinary personality,[2] making his miracles side-shows and the continuing triumphs of his spirit through the ages a progress from glory to glory. Even the books about him which continue to pour out,

1. *Von Reimarus Zu Wrede,* 1906; 3rd English Edition, A. & C. Black 1954.
2. 'I find it hard to understand how certain theologians have been able to speak doubtfully, or even slightingly, of the human greatness'—J. Knox, *The Humanity and Divinity of Christ,* CUP 1967, p. 76.

perverse and negative though many of them are,[3] testify to the power.

One title frequently attached to him might seem to link satisfactorily the Jesus of history and the Christ of faith, and that the very word we have just used, Christ, or Messiah. From New Testament times it has been used less as a title and more as a surname. The Hebrew word means 'anointed person or thing' and in consequence someone who has been anointed for office with holy oil, like the British monarch. Priests and prophets, as well as kings, were spoken of as anointed, but 'Christ' in New Testament times meant 'Son of David' or 'King of David's line'. Jesus was very cautious about such a designation. It can hardly be said that he rejected it. According to Mark he received Peter's confession, 'You are the Christ', simply with a command to silence (Mark 8:29, 30). He used his wit on the Scribes to question the title 'Son of David' (Mark 12:35 and parallels). Both 'Christ' and 'Son of David' must have suggested to contemporaries a war leader, a liberator from the Roman yoke, and that was an expectation Jesus was not going to fulfil. His Spirit and his church would conquer Rome in a different way. It looks as though our early Sunday-school lessons were right. Jesus was the Messiah but not the kind most people expected. The re-interpretation would not be complete until after Easter. But the word is too ambiguous, too cluttered, to be the central or controlling concept.

Before leaving the title 'Son of David', however, we may note that it has something in common with two other prominent titles of Jesus, 'Son of Man' and 'Son of God'. 'Son' appears in all three, linked with the genitive of another noun. Is it accidental that the church's theological word, 'Son', appears so often in the New Testament, even if in various combinations?

It appears also alone, 'the Son', mainly in St. John—

---

3. E.g. in *What About the New Testament—Essays in honour of Christopher Evans*, SCM 1975, one of the contributors addresses the revered teacher: 'I asked you . . . why you were devoting so much of your time to studying the New Testament when you considered it neither authoritative or normative, nor a primary source of faith-truth' (p. 239).

fifteen times in his gospel, all on the lips of Jesus himself, and eight times in his epistles. Much scholarship has long considered the gospel and epistles of St. John to be too late to provide evidence of the thought and speech of Jesus himself. But this usage is also found elsewhere, though less frequently. How shall we evaluate the use of 'the Son' alone or in combination, as a description or title of Jesus in the New Testament?

CHAPTER TWO

The Thunderbolt

At that time Jesus declared,
'I thank thee, Father, Lord of heaven and earth,
that thou hast hidden these things from the wise
                    and understanding
and revealed them to babes;
yea, Father, for such was thy gracious will.
All things have been delivered to me by my Father,
and no one knows the Son except the Father,
and no one knows the Father except the Son
and anyone to whom the Son chooses
                    to reveal him.'
                                (Matthew 11:25–27)

It was Karl von Hase, professor of church history at Jena, who in 1876 described this passage as 'a thunderbolt fallen from the Johannine sky'.[1] Others have varied the adjectives of the analogy and spoken of the 'Johannine thunderbolt in the Synoptic sky'. The point is that this sort of language, where Jesus addresses God, or speaks of him, as Father, and speaks of himself as Son, is prominent, indeed pervasive, in St. John's gospel, but rarer in the other three, the 'synoptics'.[2]

---

1. J. Jeremias, *New Testament Theology* Vol. I, SCM 1971, p. 56.
2. This curious expression, now a universal shorthand for the gospels of St. Matthew, St. Mark and St. Luke, is due to the fact that they, unlike St. John, can be put into a *synopsis*.

Nevertheless it appears here, and in a nearly identical parallel at Luke 10:21, 22. The two passages belong to a collection of the sayings of Jesus not found in Mark but incorporated, with variations, in Matthew and Luke. The material is referred to by the symbol Q, and its existence as a distinct source is no more than a deduction from the literary inter-relationship of the synoptic gospels.

Now it is widely held that St. John's gospel was the last of the four to be written; as J. A. T. Robinson says, 'The story of the dating of the fourth gospel in modern scholarship is an extraordinarily simple one . . . Conservatives . . . have consistently put the gospel in or about the last decade of the first century. On the other hand, the radical critics like Baur began by dating it anything up to 170 and have since steadily come down.'[3] The late dating of the gospel, even in conservative opinion, has driven a wedge between it and the historical Jesus. Its story and teaching are commonly regarded as Christian reflection on the life and person of Jesus rather than accurate reminiscence. In particular, its 'Father—Son' language is often thought to be not that of Jesus himself and perhaps even alien to Jesus' own mind and practice.

In this situation the *thunderbolt* is appropriately so called. For it demonstrates that the Father—Son language of John is to be found in the earliest (or one of the earliest) of the strata of gospel material. It is brief but unmistakable, and closest perhaps to John 5:19, 20:

> The Son can do nothing of his own accord
> but only what he sees the Father doing;
> For whatever he does
> that the Son does likewise.
> For the Father loves the Son
> And shows him all that he himself is doing.

Or again, the thunderbolt could be the briefest summary of the prayer of Jesus at John 11:41 and 17, and of the Last Discourse in John 14–16.

3. J. A. T. Robinson, *Redating the New Testament*, SCM 1976, p. 259.

The thunderbolt has been a puzzle for scholars, and 'the weight of opinion among the front-runners . . . has come down against finding here the *ipsissima verba* of Jesus.'[4] But their reasons are extraordinarily weak. The obvious similarity to John casts on it a suspicion of lateness, but 'comparison with John is a two-edged argument',[5] as we shall see. With certain scholarly comments it is difficult to be patient. Thus F. Hahn complains that it presents Jesus as arrogating to himself an exclusive position. 'Originally everyone could say 'Father', now access to the Father is tied to Jesus.'[6] Here the critic presupposes, against all the evidence, that Jesus inherited, and perhaps himself taught, a doctrine of the universal fatherhood of God.[7] Perhaps the most extraordinary case of all is that of R. Bultmann, who has dominated so much theology for the last fifty years, but who, in his *Theology of the New Testament*, never mentions these verses. Truly the selection of material is the most fundamental form of criticism and of prejudice![8]

Given the usual critical position about the respective dating of Q and St. John, a natural solution would be that 'the Johannine Father—Son theology is probably developed from a small block of early sayings tradition which Q has preserved in part at least'.[9] But the late dating of St. John's gospel has been seriously challenged by J. A. T. Robinson,[10] and the easy assumption that it is late and the last to be written can no longer be made. Moreover, the distinctive language of the thunderbolt is not completely isolated in the synoptic tradition. Its closest parallel in St. Mark's gospel is in a verse about the End, 13:32: 'But of that day or that hour no-one

4. J. D. G. Dunn, *Jesus and the Spirit*, SCM 1975, p. 28.
5. Dunn, *op. cit*. p. 28.
6. *The Titles of Jesus in Christology*, Lutterworth 1969; quoted by Dunn, *op. cit*. p. 28.
7. 'There is no ground whatever for asserting that Jesus taught a doctrine of "the Fatherhood of God and the Brotherhood of Man".' H. F. D. Sparks, 'The Doctrine of the Divine Fatherhood in the Gospels', in *Studies in the Gospels*, ed. D. E. Nineham, Blackwell 1955, p. 260.
8. See J. A. T. Robinson, *The Priority of John*, SCM 1985, p. 361.
9. Dunn, *op. cit*. p. 28.
10. *Redating the New Testament*, SCM 1976, Chapter IX.

knows, not even the angels in heaven, nor the Son, but only the Father.' It is a verse which, as the critics admit, is unlikely to have been invented because of its modesty about the position and power of the Son—something nevertheless quite consistent with St. John: 'The Father is greater than I' (John 14:28). The structure of the synoptic tradition, moreover, though it gives us nothing else quite like the thunderbolt, may be said to pre-suppose the Father—Son relationship. It is strong in the birth narratives. It is declared by the divine voice at the baptism, repeated at the transfiguration, and on the threshold of the passion appears in the parable of the vineyard, where it seems inescapable that the son in the story is an allegory of Jesus. The full implication of all this we must return to when we are clearer about the inter-relationship of the various 'Son' titles.

But for the moment we would be justified in regarding the Father—Son language of St. John as genuine reminiscence of Jesus' self-understanding. The fact that it is less explicit (apart from the thunderbolt) in the synoptics might be due to reticence or a failure of understanding. The three gospels are arrangements of teaching material in which details of the interior life of Jesus may have been thought unsuitable, though faith-fulness to the Master required a brief mention of it in his recorded sayings. That the usage was not always fully understood may well be true. Jesus often complained of his followers' lack of understanding. And, as we shall see, the existence of other forms or titles in which the word 'Son' appears does not make understanding any easier for us, as it did not for them.

CHAPTER THREE

Son of Man

The familiar usage of the gospels hides from us the strangeness of this expression, both in Greek and in English. It is normal to speak of the son of a person; a son of *man*, a common or collective noun, is not native to either language. The origin is in Hebrew and Aramaic, where 'son of man' is a literary parallel for 'man', as appears in Psalm 8:4:

> What is man that thou art mindful of him,
> and the son of man that thou dost care for him?

It appears in the vocative ('O son of man') as God's or the angel's address to Ezekiel and Daniel. Most important, however, is its occurrence in the course of the vision of Daniel 7. The judgement of God (the Ancient of Days) is pronounced on the nations and empires of the world which appear in the form of horrifying beasts, whose 'dominion was taken away'. Then

> Behold, with the clouds of heaven
> there came one like a son of man,
> and he came to the Ancient of Days
> and was presented before him.
> And to him were given dominion
> and glory and kingdom
> that all peoples, nations and languages
> Should serve him.
>
> (Daniel 7:13, 14).

'One like a son of man' means simply a man, a human figure; the beasts had been described as 'like a lion', 'like a bear', 'like a leopard'. There is little doubt that the human figure represents the people of God, Israel, man as God intended him to be, vindicated from hostile powers.

In the New Testament 'Son of Man' occurs almost exclusively on the lips of Jesus.[1] It is found fourteen times in St. Mark, thirty times in St. Matthew, twenty-three times in St. Luke and thirteen times in St. John.[2]

There is great controversy, and a voluminous literature, about every aspect of the term. Did Jesus actually use it, as the gospels say, or has it been 'read back' into his words by later Christian tradition, from circles which used the title? If Jesus did use it, did he mean himself — since he uses it in the third person—or did he mean someone else? And what, for himself or anyone else, did he mean by it?

Only a persistent scepticism can doubt that Jesus did use this term. The fact that it hardly ever appears except on his lips, and that no use is subsequently made of it, tells heavily against invention by the church. Why put something into the mouth of Jesus which had no particular meaning or interest to the custodians of the tradition? On the other hand, the survival, in the recorded words of Jesus, of terms or ideas puzzling or even unwelcome to later people is a presumption of authenticity.

Again, when he used 'Son of Man' Jesus did mean himself.[3] There is no other person in his scheme of thought it could possibly be. His third-person usage is simply a literary convention or custom of speech. It is not unusual in modern languages to find ways of avoiding or replacing the first person singular.

But if Jesus described himself as Son of Man, what did he mean by so doing? Modern scholars, after

<hr>

1. The exceptions are the final speech of Stephen (Acts 7:56) and in quotations of Psalm 8:4 (Hebrews 2:6) and Daniel 7:13 (Revelation 1:13 and 14:14).
2. J. Jeremias, *New Testament Theology* Vol. I, SCM 1971, pp. 259, 260.
3. J. D. G. Dunn, *Christology in the Making*, SCM 1980, p. 87.

surveying the confusing evidence, often conclude that, fully and precisely, we shall probably never know.

But some lines of thought we can set aside. There is a considerable development, in literature outside the canonical Old and New Testaments, of belief in 'a pre-existent divine individual called "the Son of Man" '.[4] The books called the Similitudes or Parables of Enoch and IV Ezra are the main examples of this literature. The likelihood is that these works were composed *after* the canonical gospels, and cannot therefore be quoted as having had any influence on them. Indeed, the movement may well be the other way; they may be early examples of the enterprise we are now engaged on, that is, of interpreting the 'Son of Man' usage of the gospels, in their case, misguidedly.

One thing all commentators seem to be agreed upon is that in the term 'Son of Man' the dominant substantive is the second, *man*. 'Son of Man' is no more than a literary variant of 'man'. So by it Jesus would mean himself, or himself in the frailty of the human condition, or himself as God's man, to be vindicated (as in Daniel) in due time.[5]

What never seems to be suggested[6] is that Jesus might have been equally interested, or even more interested, in the first of the two substantives, *Son*. Granted, in the Old Testament usage of the term it received no special emphasis or significance. But it is there, and Jesus often drew unconventional insights from Old Testament material. It was suggested in Chapter 2 that *Son* (not combined with any other noun) expressed Jesus' main understanding of himself. Might it not be that he used 'Son of Man' as a doublet for 'Son', employing the former especially to balance the

4. Dunn, *op. cit.* p. 75.
5. For the significance of the definite article (*the* Son of Man) in gospel usage, see C. F. D. Moule, *The Origin of Christology*, CUP 1977, pp. 11–22.
6. An exception is the French Jesuit theologian Jean Galot—'The declarations about the Son of Man imply a mysterious sonship in Jesus of divine origin' (*La Conscience de Jésus*, 1971, quoted in E. L. Mascall, *Theology and the Gospel of Christ*, SPCK 1984, p. 162).

word *man* in another part of the saying, or in contexts reminiscent of Daniel 7? Thus, in St. Mark, there are three instances where there is a balance between 'Son of Man' and 'man' or 'men' as in the literary parallelism of Psalm 8:4:

> The sabbath was made for man, not man for the sabbath, so the Son of man is Lord even of the sabbath (Mark 2:27, 28).

> The Son of man will be delivered into the hands of men (Mark 9:31).

> The Son of man goes as it is written of him, but woe is that man by whom the Son of man is betrayed (Mark 14:21).

In Mark 14:41 the actual word 'man' does not appear to balance 'Son of Man', but the saying is very close to 9:31:

> The Son of man is betrayed into the hands of sinners.

The other 'Son of Man' sayings in Mark all contain the Danielic theme of vindication after and through suffering. This is true of the two longer predictions of the passion (8:31 and 10:32–34) and of the following:

> For whoever is ashamed of me and my words in this adulterous and sinful generation, of him will the Son of man also be ashamed when he comes in the glory of his Father with the holy angels (Mark 8:38).

We might have expected 'Son' here, on the lines of Mark 13:32, 'But of that day or that hour no one knows, not even the angels in heaven, nor the Son, but only the Father.' The verb *comes*, however, seems enough, either for Our Lord or for the evangelist, to call forth 'Son of Man'.

> Then they will see the Son of man coming in clouds with great power and glory (Mark 13:26).

> And Jesus said, 'I am; and you will see the Son of
> man sitting at the right hand of Power, and coming
> with the clouds of heaven (Mark 14:62).

The first appearance of 'Son of Man' in Mark, the healing of the paralytic, has no particular suggestion of suffering and vindication—'The Son of man has authority on earth to forgive sins' (Mark 2:10). But the exercise of *authority*, and *on earth*, has strong associations with Daniel's vision, and it is perhaps worth noting that St. Matthew provides the literary parallelism. 'They glorified God, who had given such authority *to men*'. (Matthew 9:8).

If Jesus did use 'Son of Man' as a doublet for 'Son', it need not be supposed that it will alwys be completely clear to us why he uses it in any particular place; or that the gospel writers may not have interchanged them at some points, just as they do in fact interchange 'Son of Man' and the first person singular.[7]

When we turn to St. John's gospel, the same pattern emerges, though the details are quite different.[8] Of the thirteen readings, ten are in the Danielic context of lifting up, glorification, and the exercise of judgement. Two are in the 'bread of heaven' controversy in Chapter 6, where their use is related perhaps to the question, 'How can this *man* give us his flesh to eat?' (6:52). The final one is Jesus' question to the man born blind, 'Do you believe in the Son of man?' (9:35). That this occurrence of the term in a confessional or 'credal' context puzzled early readers of St. John's gospel is evident from the widespread, but inferior, reading 'Son of God'. But the precise expression Jesus used here may be less important than the dialogue of which it forms a part: 'And who is he, sir, that I may believe in him?' 'You have seen him, and he it is who speaks to you' (9:36, 37).

---

7. No less than thirty-seven times—Jeremias *op. cit.* p. 262. This goes far to account for the larger number of 'Son of Man' sayings in St. Matthew and St. Luke.
8. J. C. Fenton, *The Gospel According to John*, OUP 1970, pp. 45–6.

CHAPTER FOUR

Son of God

The problems raised by this title are quite different from those which surround 'Son of Man'. 'Son of Man' had no history *as a title* before its use by Jesus, and made little subsequent appearance in the mainstream of Christian thought, at least until the critical study of the last two centuries. 'Son of God' however had a wide currency before Jesus, both biblical and pagan, and great importance after. 'The emergence of "Son of God" as the dominant title for Christ in the fourth century was well justified by its importance in earliest christology.'[1] That is a testimony from a scholar highly sceptical of the attempt to trace the developed theology of the church back to Jesus.

Outside biblical usage, where 'god' is a common noun, sons of a god, or of the gods, abounded. Heroes or kings might claim, or be accredited with, divine ancestry (through at least one parent). The pagan centurion at the cross could give the title to Jesus without any necessary acquaintance with biblical usage (Mark 15:39).[2]

Within the Bible 'Son of God' is a term used in a number of ways. In the plural it means supernatural created beings, 'angels' in the popular sense. These are quite distinct from the Angel of Jahweh, who is God

---

1. J. D. G. Dunn, *Christology in the Making*, SCM 1980, p. 64.
2. Cf. R. H. Lightfoot, *The Gospel Message of St. Mark*, OUP 1950, p. 58.

himself in temporary human form.[3] The 'Sons of God' are capable of misbehaviour (Genesis 6:2) and are almost always spoken of in the plural. Gospel usage is unlikely to be based on this. Israel and its people corporately are called God's son; so is Israel's king, and the exceptionally righteous man. None of these usages occurs very frequently, but they give a relevant background to 'Son of God' in the gospels.

Did Jesus claim or accept the title, as the gospels represent him as doing? Sceptical critics like Rudolf Bultmann think not.[4] They point to the disparity we have already noticed in Chapter 2 between the great amount of Father—Son language in St. John's gospel and its relative paucity in the other three. But this argument depends heavily on the question of dating, and there *was* an acceptable prior use of 'Son of God' in the Old Testament which Jesus might have appropriated. It could have emphasized his role as the true Israel, or it could have been royal and messianic. Gospel wording often suggests that 'Son of God' and 'the Christ' are synonymous, interchangeable terms. Nathanael hailed Jesus, 'Rabbi, you are the Son of God! You are the King of Israel!' (John 1:49). Peter's confession was, 'You are the Christ, the Son of the living God' (Matthew 16:16). And the high priest's question was, 'Are you the Christ, the Son of the Blessed?' (Mark 14:61). There are scholars who hold that for Jesus himself the titles were not synonymous, and their identification is due to the evangelists;[5] but the evidence for this view does not seem strong.

There is a more important distinction to make. The title 'Son of God', whatever its exact meaning, by no means represents the whole of Jesus' sense of Sonship, which we have already suggested was the central and guiding idea of his life. This is not because, as is sometimes thought, 'Son of God' is a proud or presumptuous term from which the meek and lowly Jesus would shrink. On the contrary; a genitive like this means that

3. See John Thurmer, *A Detection of the Trinity*, Paternoster 1984, Chapter 2.
4. R. Bultmann, *Theology of the New Testament* I, SCM 1952.
5. E.g. O. Cullmann, in *Peter, Disciple, Apostle, Martyr*, SCM 1962.

the two nouns are separate and distinct from each other. That is partly the grammatical oddity, in English and Greek, of 'son of man'; there the son *is* man. And where 'god' is common noun (in paganism) a son of god could himself be a god. But with, say, Son of Mary, the Son is *not* Mary; and with Son of God the Son is *not* God. If 'Son of God' were all Jesus claimed for himself, or the church claimed for him, there would be no basis for the theology of Christendom. This is not to deny that Jesus may have used and accepted the term. It was right as far as it went, but it has a fatal tendency to suggest that the sonship is figurative or adoptive, which in turn implies a moment of appointment, in line with the proof-text, 'Thou art my son; Today I have begotten thee' (Psalm 2:7; cf. Acts 13:33). Sometimes it may be interchanged with 'Son of Man' (John 9:35) or 'Son'. This latter usage, where Jesus speaks of himself, or is spoken of, as 'Son', and he in turn speaks to, or of 'the Father', is quite distinct from the title 'Son of God'.[6]

The distinction appears in the epistles of St. Paul, some of which, unlike the gospels, can be dated with confidence in the 50s and are usually thought to be the earliest of the New Testament documents. St. Paul clearly accepted Our Lord's Sonship, which he refers to seventeen times. When he uses the formal title 'Son of God', there are signs that either he, or the earlier language he is taking over, thinks of this as having been conferred at the resurrection (e.g. Romans 1:4). But Paul himself is quite clear that 'Sonship' is not so limited. 'God sent forth his Son, born of a woman, born under the law' (Galatians 4:4). Sonship here is from birth, if not earlier. When he speaks of the Son, at the End, being made subject to the Father (I Corinthians 15:28), the expression might have something in common with Mark 13:32.

Likewise, a New Testament tradition independent of

6. Cf. A. J. B. Higgins, 'Some aspects of New Testament Christology'   in
Promise and Fulfilment, ed. F. F. Bruce, T. & T. Clark 1963, p. 134–5. Higgins is one of the few writers to appreciate the distinctiveness of the usage 'the Son', though he does not apparently ascribe its use to Jesus himself.

the Gospels and the letters of St. Paul, the Epistle to the Hebrews, has the magnificent opening:

> In many and various ways God spoke of old to our fathers by the prophets, but in these last days he has spoken to us by a Son, whom he appointed heir of all things, by whom also he made the worlds.

This usage, to which the diversity-in-unity of the New Testament bears witness, is our next, and central, concern.

CHAPTER FIVE

Son of the Father

This phrase, which is unique in Scripture at 2 John 3, appears in *Gloria in Excelsis*, the hymn which opens with the song of the angels at Bethlehem (Luke 2:14) and continues with acclamations of the Father and the Son by various titles. It is at least as old as the fourth century. A rather more elaborate version appears in *Te Deum*:

'Thou art the everlasting Son of the Father'.

This canticle, no doubt of similar date, echoes the great prayer of the eucharist.

'Son of the Father' might well seem, to worshippers, a tautologous and pointless expression. Who else should a son be derived from, except his mother? In fact, the acclamation catches admirably what we have claimed to be Our Lord's central insight about himself. More than 'Son of God' or 'Son of Man' it is what gave Jesus his self-understanding, which is in turn the foundation of Christian belief.

It would be improbable if the language of Jesus, especially in the 'thunderbolt' and in St. John, had *no* precedent or background. He, the greatest of creators, would have disclaimed originality in that sense. 'I do nothing on my own authority, but speak thus as the Father taught me' (John 8:28).

It has been maintained by J. Jeremias and others[1] (following the earlier suggestion of G. Dalman[2]) that the words of Jesus conceal a parable, or popular saying, about family relationships. It must always be remembered that the device of initial capital letters to help determine meaning was not available in the original, and all capital letters in our translations are interpretations by critics and translators. The definite article, moreover, in parables and similes, conveys a generic, indefinite sense. Thus the evangelists write 'the sower' (Mark 4:3 and parallels) and older versions translate it literally. Newer translations have ordinary idiomatic English— 'a sower'.

The middle lines of Matthew 11:27 could therefore be translated:

> Only a father knows his son
> and only a son knows his father.

Similarly, with Jesus' words in St. John:

> A son can do nothing by himself;
> he does only what he sees his father doing.
> (John 5:19)

And the evangelist's comment in his prologue:

> We have beheld his glory, glory
> as of a father's only son. (John 1:14)

It may be that this suggestion has appealed to scholars who wish to disprove the claim that Jesus spoke of himself as 'the Son'—a title, as we argue, more far-reaching and uncompromising than 'Son of God'. If so, the move has back-fired. As J. D. G. Dunn says, the context of the thunderbolt clearly 'applies the proverb to Jesus' own relation with the Father'.[3] In other words,

---

1. J. Jeremias, *New Testament Theology* Vol. I, SCM 1971, pp. 56ff.; C. H. Dodd, *More New Testament Studies*, Manchester UP 1968, pp. 30–40.
2. G. Dalman, *The Words of Jesus*, T. & T. Clark 1902, p. 280ff.
3. J. D. G. Dunn, *Jesus and the Spirit*, SCM 1975, p. 32.

the comparison with a human family relationship would *strengthen* the force of the thunderbolt. 'As a human son is to his father, so am I to my Father in heaven'.

Dunn's other comment is less perceptive. 'The saying which Jeremias claims to uncover' (about only a father and a son knowing each other) 'is hardly memorable, and is only of doubtful truth as a general proverb.'[4] In the experience of the modern western world it is not true at all. We suffer from the generation gap. People in other times and places are less individualistic, and expect a much greater identity between father and son—the father lives on in his son, and the son has no ambition but to be like his father. The language of Jesus, which has largely created the modern world, is itself based on the experience of the ancient world, particularly of the Old Testament.

For the moment, let us look at the way in which the synoptic gospels, which have so much less direct Father—Son language than St. John, nevertheless buttress what is present in such a way as to reduce the gulf between the two traditions.

The gospels of St. Matthew and St. Luke begin with accounts of the birth of Jesus which represent his conception as taking place without the involvement of any human male. The 'virgin birth'[5] of Our Lord touches human thought and feeling at a sensitive point, though the nature of the sensitivity has changed. Older Christianity had a bias to celibacy which it linked with the virgin birth (though the New Testament does not do so). Modern western Christianity has a bias against celibacy and often rejects the virgin birth for that reason.

The evidence for the virgin birth has often been examined. There is no clear indication of it in any other part of the New Testament, and the accounts in Matthew and Luke have few details in common. It has indeed been maintained that they do not, apart from presupposition, necessarily teach virginal conception,

4. Dunn, *op. cit.* p. 32.
5. The term 'virgin birth' is here used to mean 'virginal conception'. The doctrine that St. Mary remained *virgo intacta* after a miraculous *birth* and by subsequent celibacy is not in view.

and this is perhaps particularly true of St. Matthew.[6] On the other hand, the doctrine is firmly lodged in the Christian tradition, and until modern times only deviants questioned it.

What seems clear is that, in one way or another, it is linked with Our Lord's *Sonship*. Probably most modern scholars doubt the virgin birth as a fact, but are prepared to see it as giving expression to a claim to be 'Son of the Father'. If the genealogies aim to do this by demonstrating actual Davidic descent, then they fit awkwardly with a scheme in which Joseph, Son of David (as the angel calls him, Matthew 1:20) is not the father of Jesus. But the virgin birth has tended to eclipse the genealogies.

Tertullian, about AD 200, thought that the 'virgin birth' was essential for Jesus. 'Since he is begotten of God the Father, he is not, of course, the son of a human father'.[7] Others, including conservatives, ancient and modern, disagree. Jesus, they say, *could* have had a human father, had God so decided. For them the virgin birth is not so much necessary as 'congruous' or 'fitting'. But might Tertullian not have been right? The alternative view looks like the beginnings of rationalisation and the merging of Jesus' sonship with that of all men.

Whether the virgin birth is a story created by belief (in the divine sonship of Jesus) or a fact which helped to create the belief, rational enquiry has no means of deciding, unless other considerations, as of authority or scepticism, are made the presuppositions. However much it goes against the critical grain we must remain open to the possibility that it is fact which helped to form the doctrine in the mind of Jesus.[8] In this case

6. By a strange slip R. E. Brown says 'It is lucidly clear that Matthew believed in Mary's bodily virginity before the birth of Jesus'. (*The Virginal Conception and Bodily Resurrection of Jesus*, Chapman 1974, p. 31 n. 37). But what Matthew denied was the *paternity of Joseph* (Matthew 1:25).
7. *Adversus Marcion* 4:10.
8. The weightiest 'scientific' argument against the virgin birth is the need for God (if Jesus was to be a true human male) to create and introduce male genes. In ordinary conception, the genes on

Mary and Joseph must have imparted some knowledge of it to him. But St. Luke represents him, at the age of twelve, as understanding it better than they do (Luke 2:49, 50). If indeed they were unable to take in the fulness of the revelation, who should blame them?

The public life of Jesus began with his baptism by John. It is fruitless to attempt to isolate some historical nucleus from the accounts. The essence of them is the declaration of sonship, with which is associated the descent of the Spirit. The sonship is strengthened by the adjective *agapētos*—only, unique, beloved. It is virtually a synonym for St. John's word *monogenēs*, which appears as 'only-begotten' in the 'Nicene' creed.[9]

Peter's recognition, at Caesarea Philippi, of the status of Jesus, is dealt with in different ways by the evangelists. In St. Mark, followed largely by St. Luke, Peter says, 'You are the Christ', to which Jesus replies with a command to silence on the subject (Mark 8:27–30). In St. Matthew, however, Peter says, 'You are the Christ, the Son of the living God' (Matthew 16:16), as though the two titles were equivalent. It has been argued that they were different confessions, made at different times, and Matthew has collated them. Whether that is so or not, the language of Jesus' blessing of Peter (Matthew 16:17) picks up that of the thunderbolt. For since only a father knows his son, this confession of Jesus as Son must have been revealed to Peter by the Father in heaven. Peter's exact words, 'Son of the living God', are unique in the New Testament, and commentators do not seem to have anything illuminating to say

---

both sides 'focus the entire history of the human race'; what was the constitution of Jesus' male genes? The logic of this line of thought, however, is to make all life part of the continuing stream of nature and to deny God's power to *create*. Somehow, somewhere, God *creates*; is the virgin birth claiming more than that? See J. A. T. Robinson, *The Human Face of God*, SCM 1973, Chapter 2.

9. There is a misleading footnote in J. A. T. Robinson's *The Priority of John* (p. 397). It may be true that the idea of begetting was imported into the translation of *monogenēs* in the fourth century. But this does not affect the present argument. For the word means, not 'one of its kind' but '*only* one of its kind', 'unique'.

about them. It may be suggested tentatively that what Peter confessed, and Jesus received so enthusiastically, was not the standard title 'Son of God' (which the disciples had already used, without evoking comment, at 14:33) but a more radical understanding of sonship which this formula aims to represent.

The transfiguration repeats the declaration of sonship, with Peter, James and John now closely involved as witnesses, and in special relation to the forthcoming passion. In view of the common claim that St. John is more theological and more miraculous than the synoptics, it is interesting to note that it is they, and not St. John, who have the oracular voice making the crucial theological declaration. When St. John has a voice from heaven (12:28, 29) he comes near to providing a rational explanation of it. The crowds said it was thunder or an angel. The words, 'I have glorified it, and will glorify it again', are presumably Jesus', or John's, interpretation of the sound or the event.

Finally, the New Testament gives us a glimpse into the prayer life of Jesus. Not only did he address God in prayer as Father—itself rare and unusual; St. Mark preserves for us the Aramaic word *Abba* (14:36) which was a term of intimate family relationship. It may be that Jeremias rather overstated his case in his famous advocacy of the uniqueness of Jesus' use of *Abba* in addressing God.[10] But his main contention stands. Jesus' *Abba* was a powerful reinforcement of his sense of sonship,[11] and one in which, through the Spirit, disciples can share. St. Paul, who is not prodigal with his references to Our Lord's earthly life, twice uses the term '*Abba*, Father' (Romans 8:15, Galatians 4:6) as the

10. J. Jeremias, *New Testament Theology*, Vol. I, SCM 1971, pp. 61–8.
11. 'The equality of nature implied in the term *Abba* is expressed in Jesus' practical behaviour; he has such a familiarity with the Father that, even in his anguish and distress, he remains on the same level with him, so that he can speak with him and ask for a change in his plans'—J. Galot, *La Conscience de Jésus*, quoted in E. L. Mascall, *Theology and the Gospel of Christ*, SPCK 1984, p. 162.
12. St. Paul and St. John both carefully balance the uniqueness of Jesus' sonship with Christian participation in it. St. Paul uses the word 'sons' for Christians, but speaks of them as 'sons by

characteristic Christian address to God.[12] If, as some
have suggested, *Abba* existed before Jesus as an address
in prayer, but was low class and unacceptable as good
liturgical usage,[13] it is thoroughly characteristic of Our
Lord that he should take what this world despised and
make it of great moment; just as he took, from homely
human experience, the thought and parable of 'father
and son' to be at the centre of his life.

---

adoption' as compared with 'God's own Son'. St. John reserves
the word 'Son' for Jesus and uses other words, like 'children',
for Christians (C. F. D. Moule, *The Origin of Christology*, CUP
1977, p. 31).
13. J. D. G. Dunn, *Christology in the Making*, SCM 1980, p. 27.

What shall I do about my Son?

Jesus, we have argued, thought of himself in relation to his heavenly Father as a human son is, or ought to be, in relation to his (human) father. What actual evidence or material would give substance to this his most important parable?

Not, presumably, his childhood experience of Joseph. The gospels tell us nothing about his personal relations with Joseph, apart from the incident of the finding in the temple (Luke 2:41–51), and even there Mary seems to take the lead. Joseph evidently died before (perhaps long before) the beginning of the ministry. The matter is complicated by the question of the conception of Jesus, to which we have referred.

Jesus' interest in fathers and sons must have come from the Old Testament. Not only was this the basis of contemporary Jewish life and the primary source of the 'raw material' of the New Testament. In addition, Jesus is represented as claiming a personal and direct link with it. He spoke of what was 'written about me in the law of Moses and the prophets and the psalms' (Luke 24:44); and he said of Moses, 'He wrote of me' (John 5:46). The law or writings ascribed to Moses meant the Pentateuch, the first five books of the Bible; and 'the prophets' included what we call the historical books of Samuel and the Kings.

The historical and redaction criticism of the Old Testament is of little relevance at this point. Anyone hearing or reading it, in the form it was known to Jesus and is known to us, cannot fail to be impressed by its predominant human relationship, which is that of father and son.[1] The relationship of man and wife is secondary, no doubt partly because of the institution of polygamy, which accorded wives neither equality nor uniqueness.

In the primitive history the second story, following the Garden of Eden, is of Cain and Abel. It is true their relationship with Adam is not stressed; no doubt the story was originally an independent one. But the reader is bound to be aware that Adam, the first man, has two sons and one is murdered by the other. The pattern is set, of two sons in contrasting relation to their father. Adam's third son, Seth, is a replacement for Abel (Genesis 4:25), and of him it is explicitly said that he is a son in the image and likeness of his father Adam (Genesis 5:3). He is the youngest, or at least the youngest *named*, of the sons of Adam, and through him the human line continues. A younger (or youngest) son may sometimes be the chosen one.

The sons of Noah are not without significance. But the matter of sonship rises to a new level with Abraham,[2] who until old age achieves a son only by the handmaid Hagar (Genesis 16). The impending birth of Isaac to elderly parents is announced in the most solemn manner by the Angel of Jahweh in the form of three men (Genesis 18:1–15), and the birth has an understandably adverse effect on the position of Hagar's son Ishmael (Genesis 21:1–21); so the 'two sons' theme is taken up. The climax of the relationship of Abraham and Isaac comes in Chapter 22 with the command to

1. 'In the biblical literature there is built up upon the biological and organic relation between father and son, and upon the sociological fact of the reproduction by sons of the behaviour of their father, a vast pyramid of filial obedience'—E. C. Hoskyns and N. Davey, 'Father and Son—and the Dereliction of Jesus', in *Crucifixion—Resurrection*, SPCK 1981. This highly suggestive article is limited by its failure to refer to particular father—son relationships, and by a certain blurring of the distinction between the sonship of Jesus and that of believers in general.
2. His name means 'father', qualified in one way or another—Genesis 17:5.

sacrifice Isaac. The tension and emotion of the story must have been evident from the beginning, and it has not lessened over the years.

> Isaac said to his father Abraham, 'My Father!'
> And he said, 'Here am I, my son.'
> He said, 'Behold, the fire and the wood; but where is the lamb for a burnt offering?'
> Abraham said, 'God will provide himself the lamb for a burnt offering, my son.' So they went both of them together.
>
> (Genesis 22:7, 8).

The Roman canon of the mass treats both Abel and Abraham as precursors of Christ's eucharistic sacrifice.

In the natural course of events a son leaves his parents and becomes a father in turn. Isaac is the first biblical character to be prominent both as son and as father. He also fathers two sons, the twins Esau and Jacob, and a pretty dance they lead him (Genesis 27). Jacob, like Isaac, figures in the dual role, being first the son whose deceit and self-interest are aided and abetted by his mother, and then eventually the loving father of Joseph and Benjamin. Here the Pentateuch has its second climax in the father—son relationship. Joseph and Benjamin are the latest born, and from Jacob's best-loved wife Rachel. But Joseph and Jacob are torn apart through Jacob's favouritism and Joseph's pride. In the course of the elaborate story (Genesis 37–50) Jacob has to part with Benjamin as well, in scenes of intense emotion; but later he is happily united with his two beloved sons. Joseph is, in many ways, the paradigm of 'the son'. He indeed marries and begets children, but his role as father is much less developed; partly perhaps because he has become 'a father to Pharaoh' (Genesis 45:8). Benjamin is the most passive of sons. He never speaks, and lives solely in the love of his father and elder brother.

The events and circumstances of the Exodus concentrate on the relation of God with his people, and in this human relationships are necessarily secondary. An important connection is made, however, between the

God-centred covenant relationship and the human tie. God tells Moses, 'You shall say to Pharaoh, "Thus says the Lord, Israel is my first-born son, and I say to you, 'Let my son go that he may serve me'; if you refuse to let him go, behold, I will slay your first-born son" ' (Exodus 4:22, 23). When the threat was executed, 'there was a great cry in Egypt' (Exodus 12:30). The reader is not usually invited to have much sympathy for the Egyptians, but the hard line wavers a little at this point.

With Samuel, early interest centres on his conception. As 'son' he relates less to Elkanah and more to Eli, who addresses him thus (I Samuel 3). He was no doubt a father to his people, but his sons after the flesh were no better than Eli's. Other great men have had the same problem.

Samuel's unworthy sons are a prime reason for the establishment in Israel of the office of king, and thereby there is an exploration of the father—son relationship which matches that of Genesis. King Saul is a worthy son who becomes a bad father. His son Jonathan (most attractive of all Old Testament sons) is forced by the king's collapse to choose between his duty to his father and his love and loyalty to his friend David. The David—Jonathan saga (I Samuel 18–31) is due, we are told, to the need to show that David, as well as being anointed by God (I Samuel 16:1–13) is *also* the heir of Saul, for he is identified with Jonathan, Saul's son, and the two are merged into one personality (I Samuel 18:1–4). So, when Saul and Jonathan die in battle on Mount Gilboa, David can succeed to the kingdom in place of his 'brother Jonathan' (2 Samuel 1:26). Saul in well-disposed moments had called David his son (e.g. 1 Samuel 26:17–25).

To the modern reader the story of David and Jonathan looks like a remarkably uninhibited account of homosexual affection comparable with that of warrior companions in other traditions, like Achilles and Patroclus, Alexander and Hephaistion. How did it appear at the time of Jesus, when presumably David's status as king was felt to be sufficiently rooted in divine authority to need no justification on the ground that he was Saul's heir? Perhaps their behaviour was seen as suitable and appropriate for warrior sons who were either unmarried or often separated from their wives by military service.

David, the epic son, is also an epic father; which is a different thing from being an ideal father. Like Jacob he seems to have been guilty of favouritism and indulgence, and he suffers in consequence the full-scale military rebellion of Absalom (2 Samuel 13–19) and the usurpation of Adonijah (I Kings 1). His grief at the death of the worthless and treacherous Absalom (2 Samuel 18:33) makes it clear that a father's love is not created or constrained by merit.

David, himself a youngest son, is followed on the throne by his own youngest son, Solomon. Thereafter the kingship passes from father to son until the exile. The hereditary principle was essential to Davidic kingship and was indicated in New Testament times by the style 'Son of David'. From this material, large in quantity, rich and varied in quality, Jesus could learn by both warning and example the obedience in word and deed which was appropriate to his own sonship (Hebrews 5:8). Even the gospel genealogies (Matthew 1:1–16, Luke 3:23–38), whatever their difficulties, make the simple point of the centrality of the father—son relationship in God's providential dealings with his people, linking it to the conception of Jesus (in Matthew) and the baptism of Jesus (in Luke).

CHAPTER SEVEN

Jesus as Son

Jesus' baptism may have confirmed something already in his mind: his sonship. His role, his work, his destiny, was to be the Son, the human Son, and he had many examples and warnings to guide him. Most of those other sons married and became fathers; so their sonship receded. But Jesus was 'all son' and had no role of physical fatherhood to fulfil. Thus he is the reverse image of the treacherous and poignant Absalom, who had no son and only a stone monument to his name (2 Samuel 18:18). Jesus' name would be perpetuated by the living temple of his body (John 2:21).

As a son in his father's service, Jesus was on a military campaign in hostile territory. He knew it would be brief and he knew how it would end. There was no occasion therefore for marriage or the joys of family life. 'World-affirming' Christianity in modern days combs the gospels for hints that Jesus approved of these things, at least for others, just as earlier the ascetic tradition looked (with rather more success) for support for monasticism. But the detailed regulation of man's life in this world had been provided by the Old Testament and would be revised by his church. His own work was to fight the powers of evil, and to give direction, by inspiration, judgement and wit, to the reform of the covenant. In consequence much of his teaching was *ad hoc*; there was no comprehensive statement of doctrine or ethics, such as might aim to settle all questions and in fact be out of date in a generation, and no clearly definable stance in relation to the 'End of the world'.

The very elusiveness of Jesus, in terms of human biography, may be a pointer to his own self-understanding. Over fifty years ago a profound and devout scholar wrote,

> The form of the earthly . . . Christ is for the most part hidden from us. For all the inestimable value of the gospels, they yield us little more than a whisper of his voice; we trace in them but the outskirts of his ways.[1]

He was attacked for the supposed scepticism of these words, but much in the subsequent course of gospel study confirms them. Is it not the role of the Son to refer continually 'back' to the Father and 'forward' to the Spirit's interpretation? 'I have yet many things to say to you, but you cannot bear them now' (John 16:12). The attempt to isolate Jesus, as a human individual, simply loses him in the mist. We know him as the Son, or we do not know him at all.

A son on active service would avoid family entanglements, but he could allow himself a boon companion, in the tradition of David and Jonathan; and that he had in 'the disciple whom Jesus loved', averred by tradition to be John son of Zebedee, subsequently his most profound interpreter. Women ministered to him, and homes, like that at Bethany, were open to him. Sometimes there would be parties; there was no asceticism for its own sake, at least after the forty days' testing in the wilderness. But the apostolic band led a hard, peripatetic life, doomed to tragedy.

It is a son's duty to be a learner—primarily from his father. We need not suppose that for Jesus learning was an effortless process. As a boy he increased in wisdom and stature (Luke 2:52), and according to Hebrews he

---

1. R. H. Lightfoot, *History and Interpretation in the Gospels*, Hodder and Stoughton 1935, p. 225. As he subsequently wrote, 'It is almost a quotation from Job 26:14, to which unfortunately I omitted to give a reference, thinking that the allusion would be at once recognised . . .'—*The Gospel Message of St. Mark*, OUP 1950, p. 103 n.

learnt obedience by the things that he suffered (Hebrews 5:8)—a process the gospels give us glimpses of, at the temptations, at St. John's 'agony' (John 12:27) and in Gethsemane (Mark 14:32–42). J. A. T. Robinson holds[2] that St. John, in particular, shows traces of Jesus 'changing direction', from the influence of the Baptist, through the 'Galilean period' of healing and teaching to the servant—Son of Man who must suffer. If there is any truth in this, it is entirely in the style and spirit of sonship that its meaning and demands should be learnt gradually and perhaps painfully.

The teaching Jesus gave, especially in the synoptic gospels, centred on the kingdom he had come to fight for. In his parables he drew on human and secular material—agriculture and lifestock, business and house-keeping, parties and various forms of misbehaviour. But virtually the only *family* relationship he uses is that of father and son. Apart from the 'hidden' parable we have already noticed at Matthew 11:27 and elsewhere, the central parable about himself, the father—son relationship appears in five parables:

> The Vineyard (Mark 12:1–11 and parallels)
> The Answer to Prayer (Matthew 7:9–11 and parallel)
> The Two Sons (Matthew 21:28–32)
> The Great Supper (Matthew 22:1–10 and parallel)
> The Prodigal Son (Luke 15:11–32).

This is not an overwhelming amount of material, and in the case of the Great Supper the father—son relationship is not prominent. But teaching about his own person and status is not the main intention of the parables.

There has been a strong tendency in recent years (encouraged particularly by the work of C. H. Dodd and J. Jeremias) to refuse to ascribe to Jesus any allegorical interpretation of the parables—that is, the attaching of a specific and independent meaning to persons or events in the story. On this view, a father does not necessarily stand for God and a son does not necessarily stand for Jesus.

2. J. A. T. Robinson, *The Human face of God*, SCM 1973, pp. 81–3.

There seem reasons to modify this rule in the case of the parable of the vineyard (Mark 12:1–12 and parallels). Here there can be little doubt that in the mind of the evangelists the son stands for Jesus. Not only is he awarded (in Mark and Luke) the adjective 'beloved'; but also the opponents of Jesus perceive that he spoke the parable 'against them'—so we are given the clue. For 'wicked tenants' read 'chief priests and pharisees'. The next step is, for the owner, to read the Father; for his son, read Jesus.

Where an elaborate allegorical interpretation is provided privately after the actual parable has been told (as with the Sower and the Tares) there are grounds for thinking that the interpretation may be subsequent to the actual teaching of Jesus. The case is otherwise with the Wicked Tenants, where it is difficult to find any real story without the allegorical elements. And to say that Jesus *never* used allegory is to overwork an otherwise valuable insight.

Our present intention is to note the use of the father—son relationship in the parables with (in two cases) the common biblical theme of the two sons. One of these is that parable of parables, the Prodigal Son. It has been said[3] that this is too characteristic of St. Luke's style and language to have come from Jesus himself, and that it contains numerous Old Testament echoes, notably from the story of Joseph. It may be true that the story as we have it owes much to St. Luke's artistry and polish, but its basic theme is so close to the central interest of Jesus that there is every reason for it to have come from him. As to Old Testament allusions, Jesus was just as capable of making them as anyone else; indeed, from the argument of the previous chapter, these are what we should expect. Joseph was one of the most notable of the Old Testament's younger sons, and may have provided Our Lord with valuable insights into his own sonship. Other aspects of the Genesis story suggest details in the career of the Prodigal Son, and both sons in the parable stand in contrast to the Son who is the story-teller.

3. J. Drury, *The Parables in the Gospels*, SPCK 1985, p. 144.

CHAPTER EIGHT

Son before all worlds

Even if it is true that the claim to be Son of the Father
was made by Jesus and was central to his self-
understanding, it is true also that the documents of the
New Testament vary greatly in their treatment of it. Not
only does the incidence of the language differ consider-
ably, being much greater in St. John than elsewhere; the
style of the sonship varies also. In St. Matthew, St.
Mark and St. Luke this is expressed in terms of the
obedience and activity of Jesus as a man, and there are
signs of its origin being ascribed to a notable event—the
baptism or the virgin birth. In St. John the Son appears
to be an eternal being who has come temporarily to earth
but who will return to heaven, mission accomplished.
In St. Paul and the Epistle to the Hebrews both ways of
thinking can be found, depending often on how we
interpret the language.

It is common to arrange the New Testament books in
their supposed order of writing, and to conclude that,
since the pre-existence of Jesus is found only in the
latest strata, the concept cannot be attributed to Jesus
himself. St. John's gospel and subsequent Christian
theology therefore face the charge of being alien to Jesus'
self-understanding; and, moreover, of proclaiming a
Jesus who is not truly human, because he claims pre-
existence and awareness of a heavenly life not given to
mortal man. An impressive form of this argument
appears in J. D. G. Dunn's book *Christology in the
making*.

As we have already said, arguments from the supposed dating of New Testament books are hazardous. It
is clear also that, although they do not deal with pre-
existence, the synoptic gospels present a very high
claim for Our Lord. As Dunn says, 'The christology of a
sonship distinctive in its sense of intimacy and unique
in its consciousness of eschatological significance . . . can
only be called a *high christology*—higher certainly than a
christology of a righteous man or a charismatic exorcist,
higher perhaps than that of a Davidic Messiah.'[1]
'Official' church theology has sometimes played down
the humanity of Jesus and presented him as a being
from another world who only appeared to be human
(the heresy called docetism[2]). The part played by
biblical scholarship in recovering the humanity of Our
Lord should be gratefully acknowledged—though that
recovery was begun in the far-reaching changes of the
western middle ages.[3] An essential characteristic of
Jesus' sonship was being human. We have argued that
in the synoptic gospels, no less than in the rest of the
New Testament, Jesus claims to be Son of the Father.
The essence of this claim is relationship, not origin;[4] an
eternal Father implies an eternal Son, but the implication
is not drawn out, at least as regards pre-existence. In St.
John it is drawn out; so much so that we could make the
mistake of thinking the Son not only eternal but
inhuman. He speaks of what he has seen with his
Father (8:38), and of the glory he had with his Father
before the world was made (17:5). If one started off with
the idea of a pre-existent individual divine Son, who, as
one of a heavenly family, was sent to earth, it would be
natural to interpret such expressions in that way. But
neither Jesus nor John did so think.

1. *Op. cit.* pp. 32, 33.
2. From the Greek verb *dokein*, to seem, to appear.
3. The 'twelfth-century renaissance'—see G. L. Prestige, 'Eros; or
   Devotion to the Sacred Humanity', in *Fathers and Heretics*, SPCK
   1940; and C. Morris, *The Discovery of the Individual*, SPCK 1972.
4. E. L. Mascall has drawn attention (in *Theology and the Gospel of
   Christ*, SPCK 1984) to the thought of Jean Galot, who develops
   Augustine's concept of person as 'relational being' and applies
   this both to the persons of the Trinity and to the person of the
   Son in the incarnation; see below, Chapter 11.

There are two contrasted ways of approaching the mystery of God's being. One is to start with the unity, the oneness, of God, which is nevertheless apprehended by us in diverse aspects or 'persons'. This style or tradition is called *monist* or *monarchian*. The other starts with the distinction of persons and sets out to explain and reconcile God's unity with them—an approach called *pluralism*. We are apt to approach St. John's language with a pluralism he would not have recognized. When Jesus speaks of pre-existence, he is identifying himself with the great attributes of God, his Word and his Wisdom. His language echoes the claims of Wisdom in the Old Testament:

> Ages ago I was set up,
> At the first, before the beginning of the earth . . .
> When he established the heavens
> > I was there . . .
> Then I was beside him, like a master
> > workman
> And I was daily his delight,
> Rejoicing before him always.
> > (Proverbs 8:23, 27, 30)

Jesus can speak of his pre-existence as Wisdom can speak as a 'person' separate from God. But Wisdom is not separate from God; it is a hallowed and forceful way of speaking of his being and work. A *monarchian* view of God lies behind the New Testament, and should control our understanding of its language. Christians reflecting on the fact of Jesus may have been impelled to a greater pluralism, for Jesus' Father—Son understanding is of a plurality of persons.[5] Both monism and pluralism were (and are) capable of mistakes and exaggerations, but neither has ever triumphed finally over the other, and both remain available, with due caution, to Christian thought.

An achievement of pluralism appears in the work of Origen (c.185–254), in his day the church's most

5. For the importance of the word 'person' see J. Thurmer, *A Detection of the Trinity*, Paternoster 1984, Chapter 6.

impressive thinker since the New Testament writers. In his handling of the father—son analogy, Origen makes the important contribution that the Son was not (as would be the case with human beings) begotten at a point in time, so that whereas with a human son there is a time when the father exists without him, with God this is not so. The Son is 'eternally begotten', 'begotten by an eternal act'. Origen had in fact hit on the essential point to defend the 'Father—Son' doctrine of Jesus and the New Testament. This is true of all the biblical evidence we have surveyed. Occasionally (as with Abraham and Isaac) the circumstances of the begetting are important. But they tell us nothing about the begetting of the eternal Son, because that is not the purpose of the analogy. Jesus is to his heavenly Father as a human son to a human father *in their adult relationship.* Origen, the legacy of whose theology was dubious in other respects, never had a better thought than this. With the eternity of the Son is closely connected his agency in creation. St. Paul's statement of this in his epistles is remarkable not only for the earliness of so dramatic an assertion, but also for the apparent absence of any controversy about it. It is sometimes suggested that he is quoting existing hymns or slogans, which would of course make the doctrine even earlier. The first reference is in the discussion about 'idol meat':

> For us there is one God, the Father, from whom are all things and for whom we exist, and one Lord, Jesus Christ, through whom are all things and through whom we exist. (I Corinthians 8:6).

In a later epistle, it is more developed:

> (The Son) is the image of the invisible God, the first-born of all creation; for in him all things were created, in heaven and on earth . . . all things were created through him and for him.
> (Colossians 1:15, 16)

As we have already said of the language of St. John, St.

Paul is not here proclaiming the pre-existence of Jesus as an individual separate from God. He is identifying Jesus with the activity, especially the wisdom, of God, as manifested in creation. The Epistle to the Hebrews does the same. 'God has spoken to us by a Son . . . through whom he created the world' (Hebrews 1:2). The synoptic gospels do not refer explicitly to the Son's work in creation, but St. Matthew aligns him to the Wisdom of God, which, as we have seen, is the basis of thought for his eternity. It is St. John in his prologue who gives definite expression to the Son in creation, in verses which, more than any others, have been the foundation of Christian theology.

> In the beginning was the Word, and the Word was with God, and the Word was God. He was in the beginning with God; all things were made through him, and without him was not anything made that was made. . . . And the Word became flesh, and dwelt among us, full of grace and truth; we have beheld his glory, glory as of the only Son from the Father (John 1:1–3, 14).

It is sometimes suggested that these verses about the Word already existed as a confession of faith, and that St. John made them the beginning of a 'second edition' of his gospel. The dovetailing of them into the account of John the Baptist shows some signs of awkwardness. In any case, the insight present in St. Paul is here given clear statement as the prologue to a gospel, and the divine attribute selected is the Word. St. John does not claim that Jesus called himself the Word, and this itself is confirmation of his historical trustworthiness; if he were putting into Jesus' mouth truths subsequently apprehended by Christians, 'I am the Word' would be very appropriate. But in v. 14 he ties his creed closely to Jesus' self-understanding. What we have beheld is his glory (in the sense of 'image') *as of a father's only son*. The definite articles and consequent capital letters in our translations have no basis in the Greek.[6] Of modern

6. See J. A. T. Robinson, *The Priority of John*, SCM 1985, p. 321.

English versions, only J. B. Phillips translates it correctly. St. John, in a prologue which confessedly represents his, or the church's reflection, introduces also the Lord's own parable of his essential self-understanding.

The 'I am' sayings which *are* attributed to Jesus may seem to have an immodest ring about them. The words suggest a translation of the divine name of the Old Testament. It is difficult to believe that Jesus' usage does not include at least a hint of that name, which, like everything else, Jesus has from his Father ('thy name which thou hast given me', John 17:11 and 12). The 'I am' sayings with a predicate are stylised in, and characteristic of, St. John's gospel, but they have a parallel in the synoptics; particularly, perhaps, the 'I say to you' of the Sermon on the Mount (Matthew 5:22 etc.). The interesting suggestion has been made that the 'I' here has something in common with that of the mystics, conscious of a high degree of identification with the grace of God.[7] For Jesus it is the 'I' of the Eternal Son, who receives the Name, and embodies the Word and Wisdom of the Father, and who can say 'I and the Father are one' (John 10:30). In this connection, it is significant that in the synoptic gospels Jesus is condemned by the Jewish council for blasphemy (Mark 14:64 and parallels). This puzzles commentators, for the words attributed to Jesus do not seem to amount to blasphemy in contemporary understanding, and there is doubt about the possibility of knowing exactly what was said. But is it not likely that the subtlety of Jesus' claim, which has stretched the minds of men for two thousand years, could be represented by the ill-disposed as blasphemy? That is exactly what St. John reports; 'We stone you for no good work but for blasphemy; because you, being a man, make yourself God' (John 10:33).

But did he, in fact, claim to be God? Put simply, conventional orthodoxy thinks he did and modern scholarship thinks he did not. They are both wrong. What Jesus claimed, consistently, was to be Son of the Father. St. Thomas could say to him, 'My Lord and my God' (John 20:28) and be heard with the silence of

7. J. A. T. Robinson, *op. cit.* pp. 387–8.

consent. But he never says of himself, 'I am God'; his God is the Father (John 20:17); but his claim is to be God *in the manner of the incarnate Son.*[8] That is why a doctrine of the Trinity, implicit or explicit, is central and essential to the experience and teaching of Jesus. It is not a secondary dogma unrelated to practical discipleship. A systematised doctrine, handled by the unoriginal and unimaginative, may easily seem in sharp contrast to the fresh, vigorous and paradoxical insight of Jesus; but that is quite a different thing from there being an essential conflict or discontinuity between them.

8. Or, as Bishop Frank Weston liked to say, 'God in manhood'; F. Weston, *The One Christ*, Longmans 1914.

CHAPTER NINE

Of one Substance

When Christianity went out into the Greek and Roman world, the ambiguity of the title 'Son of God', which we have already noticed (Chapter 4), was writ large. It would not be an exaggeration to say that the church's main doctrinal concern, in the first four centuries, was to establish the true interpretation. This concern was complicated by the two contrasting ways of approaching the mystery of God's being, as we saw in the last chapter. In these centuries a pluralist view was strong, especially in the Greek east; but monarchianism still had supporters, especially in the Latin west. The tension between the two approaches meant that when the crisis came the issues were not clear-cut.

The adversary who forced the church to make up its mind was the Alexandrian presbyter Arius, whose controversial views troubled both church and state a few years after the end of the great persecution. Doctrinal disagreements in the early church were not handled with gentlemanly decorum, and the opponents of Arius spoke of him with a violence that has often been repeated down to the present day. Some of the vituperation can hardly be read without a smile, and it plays into the hands of modern sceptics: 'A mass of presumptuous theorizing, supported by alternate scraps of obsolete traditionalism and uncritical text-mongering . . . a lifeless system of unspiritual pride and hard unlovingness.'[1]

1. H. W. Gwatkin, *Studies of Arianism*, Bell 1900, p. 274. Cf.

It is indeed true that the Arian system was the effective negation of Christianity. It proclaimed the philosopher's god, one, remote, and utterly detached from men and from the world—the type of God, nevertheless, whom many want to believe in, both then and since. The crux of the scheme, however, and what condemned it, was its handling of the Father—Son analogy. Jesus could not be, for Arius, equal to or identified with God—that would compromise God's uniqueness and his detachment from the world. Aware that 'Son of God' in the Bible could mean Israel, or the king, or even a good man, Arius applied the term 'Son' to Jesus in the same way. 'Son' and 'God' were courtesy titles, for Jesus was a creature, begotten in the figurative sense of being made or created.[2] Consequently, he had a beginning. Since he was the first of creatures, this was before time, so it would be incorrect to say 'There was a time when he was not.' But it is essential to Arianism to say 'There was when he was not', otherwise he would be eternal, an attribute of the Father alone.[3] So in the 'time before time' the Son came into being. For Arius, moreover, the Son had no real communion with God or inherent knowledge of him.

It is common to say of Arius that he was over-literal. But in a sense he was not literal enough. He overthrew the father—son analogy, central as it is to the New Testament.[4] The one important use he makes of it is a mistaken one—that is, to focus on the temporal nature of the act of begetting, which is not the point of the

---

M. F. Wiles, 'In defence of Arius', in *Working Papers in Doctrine*, SCM 1976.

2. 'The basic Arian tactics consisted in accepting the language of orthodoxy but giving it a lower currency value'—M. F. Wiles, *art. cit.* p. 24.

3. 'They venture to say, "How can the Son always exist with the Father? For men come from men, and are sons, after a time; and the father is thirty years old when the son begins to be, being begotten; and in short of every man it is true that he was not, before his generation" '—Athanasius, *Contra Arianos* 2:34.

4. ' "Sonship" is in the last resort a relationship of a human being to God'—G. W. H. Lampe, *God as Spirit*, OUP 1977, p. 139. A great deal of heresy, ancient and modern, is concentrated in that sentence.

analogy. Even this he compromised by accepting the contemporary confusion of 'begetting' and 'creating'.

For some time a number of other theologians had been avoiding the ambiguities of the term 'Son' and concentrating on 'Word'. Athanasius (Archbishop of Alexandria 328–373) wrote a treatise *On the Incarnation of the Word of God*, either just before or soon after the conflict with Arius, and he uses 'Son' in it only a handful of times. Arius, on the other hand, disliked calling Jesus the 'Word'. It is not difficult to see why Athanasius liked 'Word' more than 'Son' and Arius liked 'Son' more than 'Word'. A man can exist without his son, but he can hardly exist without his word.

The intervention of Arius made the church act. By 325 Constantine, a Christian catechumen, was sole Emperor, and, aghast at the bitterness of the quarrel over Arius, he lectured the disputants by letter, urging them to give up fighting over mere words and mysteries beyond our understanding and return to the common task. Such exhortations addressed to aroused partisans and coming from authority wanting a quiet life had no more effect then than they would have today.

At the Council of Nicea in 325 Constantine presided. The Council adopted a baptismal creed[5] which, with amendments and appended anathemas (forbidden opinions), decisively banned the doctrines of Arius. It stated that the Son was 'begotten not made', and by denying the Arian slogan, 'There was when he was not', it secured Origen's insight of eternal generation. But the Council went further. At Constantine's urging it described the Son as 'of one substance', consubstantial, *homo-ousios* with the Father. Arius had opposed this and attacked this very word, his supporters then and since pointing out (with fury) that it was not biblical. Many modern biblical scholars also cannot restrain their indignation, claiming that the use of the category of substance had nothing in common with the New Testament or with Jesus' self-understanding.[6] But in

5. This is not the 'Nicene creed' familiar for many centuries at the Eucharist, but they have crucial expressions in common. The Eucharistic creed came from later councils.
6. In contrast, at the end of his study (published posthumously) of

essence all the council fathers did (and it was no small achievement) was to secure the true interpretation of Jesus' own analogy. If he was to his heavenly Father as a human son is to a human father, then it must be made clear that this means *relationship*, not origin, and equality, as of a father and his actual (not figurative) son. Analogies, even Our Lord's, can be misunderstood —look at the fate of the parables! When this happens, simply to repeat the analogy is not sufficient. It must be defined to exclude error. Achieving this may call for new terminology, and this must be found from the language the church and the world is speaking at that time. Being biblical does not mean using biblical words; it means being faithful, with whatever words are necessary, to the truth the Bible expresses.

Not that the Nicene word *homoousios* solved all problems—far from it. For it contains a *double entendre* which did not hinder its effective use against Arius, but which made it highly suspect in the years following the Council. The ambiguity is unresolvable because it corresponds to the two approaches to the being of God described in Chapter 8. The Greek word *ousia* had a variety of meanings. The compound adjective *homoousios* meant 'made of the same stuff',[7] of the same species. This is almost certainly the sense in which it was used at Nicea, with a rider that it was not to be understood in a physical or material way—be careful of your analogies! Thus it expressed, for the Son, his equality, but not his identity, with the Father.[8]

The term can, however, in both ancient and modern usage, mean 'identity of substance', and it was in this sense, by a verbal accident like the presence of the word 'son' in 'Son of Man', that it came to be interpreted. That was so unpleasing and unacceptable to a large body of eastern pluralists that Arianism made a comeback. The renewed danger was overcome by the patient

---

St. John's gospel, J. A. T. Robinson wrote, 'John is not at all far from the central and essential affirmation of Jesus' "consubstantiality" with God'—*The Priority of John*, SCM 1985, p. 396.
7. G. L. Prestige, *God in Patristic Thought*, Heinemann 1936, p. 197.
8. See J. N. D. Kelly, *Early Christian Doctrines*, A. & C. Black 1965, pp. 223–237.

and painstakingly work of Athanasius in explaining the different languages and traditions to each other, so preventing a schism between Latin monarchians and Greek pluralists.

The ambiguity of 'consubstantial' raises an important point about the father—son analogy. We would have no difficulty in accepting a father and son as of *the same species*; no one would dream of thinking otherwise. What man begets is man; what God begets is God. But the alternative, and more radical, meaning of 'consubstantial' picks up that element in the biblical father—son relationship which is strange to modern ears. Father and son in the Bible are a corporate personality, a 'one flesh' no less than man and wife, in which the father extends his life and work through his son and the son executes his father's will. Where sin or circumstance thwarts or contradicts this, the result is not just the clash of personality that the flesh is heir to—it is a death of the corporate personality and a living death for the individual father or son, choosing, or forced, to live a life against their nature. Jesus' father—son parable is for all times and places. But like his other parables, it draws particularly on the setting of his own time and place, which we must know, as far as mind and imagination can take us.

CHAPTER TEN

Son and Spirit

We have argued throughout that 'Son of the Father' represented Jesus' self-understanding, and we have drawn out some of the meaning of this phrase, for Jesus, for the New Testament writers and for the later church. This is not to deny he called himself, or was called, other things as well as Son—Son of Man, Son of God, Holy One of God, Christ. St. John calls him the Word (John 1:14) but never suggests that Jesus spoke thus of himself. Does Jesus' understanding of God and of himself require any third term—one which is not an alternative to Father or Son?

In St. Paul and St. John the answer is clearly yes—the Spirit is linked with the Father and the Son as the third (and final) term of the divine mystery. Other parts of the New Testament are less explicit.

Spirit is a prominent Old Testament word, but it has none of the human and family associations of father and son. From its basic meaning of 'wind' or 'breath' it comes frequently to imply the power or influence of God, especially as contrasted with man in his ordinary state. It was the Spirit of the Lord which came upon Saul (I Samuel 10) and David (I Samuel 16) at their anointing and possessed the prophet of good news (Isaiah 61:1). It is not without human reference, for a man has spirit, or a spirit. The attributes of God in the Old Testament all bear some analogy with the activity and psychology of man. Thus the sons of the prophets could say, 'The spirit of Elijah has settled on Elisha' (2 Kings 2:15).

If we compare the treatment of spirit in the gospels of St. Matthew and St. Mark with that in St. John, we find a contrast broadly similar to that in the case of sonship. St. John has full and frequent references to the spirit, where St. Matthew and St. Mark have few. Nevertheless they are weighty and closely connected with sonship. Mary was found to be 'with child of the Holy Spirit' (Matthew 1:18). In both accounts of the baptism Jesus saw the Spirit descending as a dove (Matthew 3:16; Mark 1:10) before or at the moment of his proclamation as Son by the divine voice. In both it is the Spirit who drives Jesus into the wilderness (explicitly, in Matthew, to test his sonship). In both Jesus by the Spirit carries out exorcisms of demons who know of his sonship. 'If it is by the Spirit of God that I cast out demons, then the Kingdom of God has come upon you' (Matthew 12:28).[1] Both have the profound and puzzling saying about the sin against the Holy Spirit (Matthew 12:31, 32; Mark 3:28, 29) contrasted (in Matthew) with blasphemy against the Son of Man.[2] Matthew ends his gospel with the risen Lord's command to baptize 'in the name of the Father, and of the Son, and of the Holy Spirit' (Matthew 28:19). There is every reason why Our Lord should have used such a formula, and if St. Mark's gospel had an original ending which has been lost, it could have appeared there also. What better way to end a gospel which began with a baptism proclaiming Jesus as the Son indwelt by the Spirit?

1. St. Luke has 'finger of God' here and there is no way of being sure which is the more authentic. There is no difference of meaning. The variation draws attention once again to the 'analogous' nature of language about God.
2. Has 'Son of Man' replaced 'Son' here through the proximity of 'men' or 'sons of men'? Cf. Chapter 3. If so, the structure of the saying is trinitarian, viz. 'God (the Father) will forgive sin against the Son, but not against the Spirit'. Sin against the Spirit can hardly be a specific act or acts; it must be a forceful but oblique way of describing some state in which forgiveness cannot operate, like the hardened heart or the closed mind. 'When scrupulous people torment themselves about whether they have committed the unforgiveable sin, . . . the fact that they are worrying about it is the strongest evidence that they have not committed it'—A. M. Ramsey, *Holy Spirit*, SPCK 1977, p. 30.

St. Luke has most of the references to the Spirit found in St. Matthew and St. Mark, and more. In addition, he has a whole companion volume, the Acts of the Apostles, with the Spirit as the hero, given to the disciples on the day of Pentecost (Acts 2:1–4) and guiding the church's proclamation of the Son from Jerusalem to Rome.

It is however St. John who makes most explicit the person and work of the Spirit, as he does the sonship of Jesus. The Son, himself sent by the Father, will send the Spirit from the Father (John 15:26), and the Spirit will declare the things of the Son to us (John 16:13–15). The full availability of the Spirit awaits the glorification of the Son (John 7:39). Hence the Spirit is bestowed, perhaps at the death of Jesus (19:30); certainly after his resurrection (20:22).

Apart from its inherent meaning as an attribute or aspect of God, the choice of the word Spirit to accompany Father and Son is of great importance. Father and Son have, as we have seen, an inevitable family reference. We might expect a further term to be of the same kind—mother, daughter, grandson? A quite different and intangible word tells us that the 'family' reference of Father and Son must be qualified with other truths. They do not start a genealogy or expand into a crowd. Father and Son, as we have already seen, are a corporate personality some way removed from our modern experience of fathers and sons, and 'Spirit' may be indicative of the unity of the Father and the Son. But the word itself is too intangible to be a satisfactory *icon* of God, as art and devotion always discover. There is no fourth, or subsequent term. Jesus was quite clear that he was the second of three.[3]

In Christian reflection and definition the Spirit has generally lagged behind the Father and the Son, and

---

3. There are examples in modern theology of a quite different evaluation of 'Spirit' as the controlling concept of deity. Such an approach undermines Our Lord's Father—Son understanding and the doctrine of the Trinity. See, e.g. G. W. H. Lampe, *God as Spirit*, OUP 1977, and M. F. Wiles, 'The Holy Spirit in Christian Theology', in *Explorations in Theology 4*, SCM 1979.

this is neither surprising nor discreditable. Jesus' primary self-understanding was as Son of the Father, a human analogy inviting and receiving rational exploration. It is the Son, as the express image of the Father, who is the focus of our love, worship, thought and art. It is the Spirit's business to strengthen and encourage that relationship, not to rival it. Gregory of Nazianzus, towards the end of the fourth century, produced a rather dubious doctrine of development, by which the persons of the Godhead were revealed successively— the Father in the Old Testament, the Son in the New, and the Spirit in the church. That is certainly not an acceptable view of the relation of the covenants. It is the incarnate Son who names and identifies the three persons after the groundwork of the men of old. But Gregory is right to find it appropriate that the Spirit's *doctrine* should be late in time.

Towards the end of his life Athanasius recognised and taught that the Spirit was consubstantial with the Father and the Son. None of the other possibilities which were being canvassed was acceptable. He judged, and the Church judged with him, that if the teaching of the Lord was to be understood and preserved, the *homo-ousion* of the Spirit was as necessary as that of the Son.

Once again, the handling of the analogy was crucial. Opponents of Athanasius asked how a consubstantial Spirit was to be fitted in to the family analogy. Was he without origin (a second Father was too bizarre), or, more likely, a second Son; had the Son a brother? The younger contemporaries of Athanasius, the 'Cappadocians' Basil the Great, Gregory of Nazianzus and Gregory of Nyssa, struggled with this challenge. Gregory of Nyssa, in particular, distinguished the three persons by their origin, and distinguished the Spirit from the Son in terms of a different relationship to the Father.

The consubstantiality of the Spirit was affirmed by the Council of Constantinople in 381 and was not seriously challenged thereafter. It was not apparently sufficiently controversial to need including in the Eucharistic creed, though it appears in *Quicunque Vult*, a fifth-century canticle known as the Athanasian creed but embodying the teaching of Augustine rather than

Athanasius. This also contains a form of the distinction of the persons:

> The Father is made of none, nor created, nor begotten.
> The Son is of the Father alone; not made nor created but begotten.
> The Holy Ghost is of the Father and the Son; not made, nor created, nor begotten, but proceeding.

The rather colourless word 'proceeding' draws attention to the absence, for the larger part of Christian history, of any positive and satisfactory analogy of the Spirit in human experience. Father and Son have had, from the beginning, their rich reference to human relationship. But there is no way forward on those lines for the understanding of the Spirit. If the three terms, Father, Son and Spirit are to be interpreted dynamically and practically, another analogy is needed to set alongside that of father and son, taking into account the corporate personality we have seen that our Lord's usage implies.[4]

Modern preachers and commentators commonly say that the doctrine of the Trinity, however difficult to understand, results from Christian experience—that the church was obliged, by the very fact of its relationship with God, to make the distinction of persons. This claim is dubious. There is little in the history of the early church to suggest that the status and role of the Spirit, as distinct from the exalted Son, was a matter of sheer experience.[5] It was produced by the teaching of Jesus, which the church rightly recognized to be the source, guide and goal (Romans 11:36 NEB) of its experience.

4. See J. Thurmer, 'The Analogy of the Trinity' in the *Scottish Journal of Theology*, Vol. 34, pp. 509–515; and *A Detection of the Trinity*, Paternoster 1984, Chapter 7.
5. 'The ante-Nicene fathers did not adopt a Trinitarian scheme of thought about God because they felt themselves compelled to do so as the only rational means of explanation of their experience . . . (but) because it was the already accepted pattern of expression'.—M. F. Wiles, *Working Papers in Doctrine*, SCM 1976 p. 11. In Wiles' view this makes the Trinity 'an arbitrary analysis of the activity of God . . . not of essential significance' (p. 15). In fact it puts the authority for the doctrine back where it belongs, in the thought and words of Jesus.

CHAPTER ELEVEN

The Human Form Divine

The course of doctrinal development in the early church is rather like the progress of modern medical science, where diseases are identified and eliminated, but we then die of something else—of some condition largely concealed by earlier maladies. The Council of Nicea's definition of the Son as consubstantial with the Father brought forward the questions 'How, and in what sense is he man?'. This was argued in the church with a fury which exceeded that of the earlier conflict, and is widely considered to have received less satisfactory resolution. There was no-one of the stature of Athanasius to grapple with it, and where protagonists like Cyril and Nestorius are concerned it is less easy to be confident that orthodoxy has drawn the right line between 'fathers' and 'heretics'.

The two main approaches centred on the outlook of the patriarchal sees of Antioch and Alexandria respectively, and they constituted an early example of 'party spirit' in the church—to be followed by realists and nominalists, papalists and imperialists, Jesuits and Jansenists and many others. A sympathetic observer, looking back, finds it hard to say the right was all on one side. Yet in its own day each party must have seemed, in relation to its opponent, the complete expression of human and divine truth, and worth living and dying for.

The Alexandrians thought that the Eternal Son, the

divine Word or *Logos*, 'took flesh' in the incarnation. Their Jesus tended to be human only in a formal and honorific sense. They could explain the unity of his person, but not his humanity. Where the New Testament speaks of, or assumes, human frailty or vulnerability in Jesus, they were inclined to explain it away in a manner which is to us both unconvincing and unedifying. The heretical extreme of the Alexandrians was docetism, and Apollinarius, who denied that Jesus had a human *mind*, was typically Alexandrian in his approach.

The Antiochenes, on the other hand, insisted on the full humanity of Jesus and were encouraged by their literal interpretation of scripture. But they tended to give their redeemer a dual personality, and their opponents claimed that they preached not 'one Lord Jesus Christ' but two—the eternal Son and the human Jesus in a 'business partnership'.[1]

The Christian church was now bound up with the Roman Empire, its government and internal tensions, and the theology of Antioch and Alexandria each acquired political and cultural expression. Advantage was achieved, now by one side, now by the other in a march of events which was dramatic, complex and often unedifying.

In 451 the Council of Chalcedon achieved a definition which occupies in church history a position comparable to that of Nicea. The Council confessed

> One and the same Son, our Lord Jesus Christ, perfect in Godhead, perfect in manhood, truly God and truly man . . . consubstantial with the Father as regards Godhead, and consubstantial with us as regards manhood, like us in all things apart from sin . . . one and the same Christ, Son, Lord, only begotten, in two natures without confusion, without change, without division, without separation; the difference of the natures being in no way removed because of the union, but rather the property of each nature being preserved and coming together into one person and one *hypostasis* . . .

1. G. L. Prestige, *Fathers and Heretics*, SPCK 1940, p. 239.

The definition represented a swing against earlier Alexandrian successes, and was not universally acceptable, being the formal cause of a schism which remains unhealed to this day. Its subsequent interpretation was weighted in an Alexandrian direction, notably by the Second Council of Constantinople, 553, which formally authorized Cyril of Alexandria's doctrine of *anhypostasia*, that is, that Our Lord had human nature but not a human personality; he was man, but not a man; his personality was that of the Eternal Son. Christian orthodoxy in the past accepted the doctrine without a murmur, as do modern conservative scholars like Barth and Brunner. Others, however, cannot contain their fury. J. A. T. Robinson calls it 'astonishing . . . so strange and so remote both from common sense and from scripture that it requires a considerable effort of the imagination to understand what can even have been meant by it, let alone why it has been so generally regarded as essential'.[2] It is a widely-held judgement that 'impersonal humanity' robs Our Lord of any true humanity. No doubt our increasing awareness of the complexity of human personality, and of the 'human' element in the gospels, contributes to modern sensitivity on this matter. Robinson doubts whether the Chalcedonian definition itself really secures Our Lord's humanity, because although it speaks of him as 'consubstantial' with us, it at once adds the phrase 'like us (apart from sin)'. The adjective 'like' (*homoios*) had been rejected as a description of the relationship of the Father and the Son, and its use here could be considered docetic; Christ was 'like man' but *not* man. This, however, seems clearly unfair to the fathers of Chalcedon. Their phrase 'like us, apart from sin' is a close reference to Hebrews 4:15 (a point Robinson does not mention) and is designed to give scriptural backing to the humanity they have claimed for Christ.

Much of the dislike of 'impersonal humanity' surely stems from the assumption of modern psychology that the essential human unit is the self-conscious individual.

2. J. A. T. Robinson, *The Human Face of God*, SCM 1973, pp. 105, 106.

Nothing else is human, so if Jesus is not that, he is not human. But many modern discussions show the abstraction and unreality which they lay at the door of Chalcedon. Much of our practice and experience is not individualistic at all. We all, to a greater or less degree, act as a part of a larger unit—national, religious, cultural, or wherever we 'belong' by taste or interest or accident—and when we do so we have, or deploy, no personality of our own. Would anyone say that in such a state we are not human? If he did he would disown a great deal of human activity. It is commonly observed that in such a group or collective personality people can be dramatically better or worse than they would be individually. But the point at the moment is not to assess the capacity, for good or ill, of the corporate personality, but simply to note its existence. We can be, and very often are, human without an individual human personality being in charge of each one of us.

Our Lord's human nature has seemed to defy definition. But is it not to be understood as in the common expression, often used in exasperation or extenuation, 'it's human nature'—the physical, mental and psychic raw material we all share, and which awaits direction by personality, individual or corporate? So understood, we know a good deal about Christ's human nature. Partly it is the inheritance of Adam common to the whole human race; partly it is that of a Jew at that particular time and place. But what gave him his unique individual direction, coherence and personality was the Word or Son of the Father.

Various modern attempts have been made, some very impressive, to go further than this and soften the element of paradox. The doctrine of Leontius of Byzantium (c. 485–543), which he called *enhypostasia*, has been revived.[3] According to this, the Son was peculiarly suitable to 'operate' the flesh of Christ because, by virtue of God's creation of man in his own image, human personality was inherently part of him. Archbishop Temple approved of this. 'The human personality of Jesus Christ is subsumed in the Divine Person of the

3. H. M. Relton, *A Study in Christology*, SPCK 1917.

Creative Word.'[4] If the object is to prove that Jesus had an *individual human personality* it is difficult to see that this helps much; to be subsumed in this way is not the common lot of humanity, and 'subsume' is one of those words which conceals, rather than reveals, thought. But it is salutary to be reminded that the eternal Son is not an abstraction or an alien from outer space, but the Word of the Father who now fulfils his purpose of love and takes man his creature to his heart. The incarnation must not be treated in isolation from the Trinity. 'Incarnability' is a property of the Son, defining his personality in relation to the Father and the Spirit.[5]

Archbishop Temple also puts the question (unreal and abstract though he agrees it is), 'What would be left if the divine Word were withdrawn from Jesus?', and answers, 'Not nothing at all, but a man.'[6] The crucial subsequent question then is, 'What sort of a man?' and this he neither asks nor answers. For if the answer is a typical, ordinary man, we have the Nestorian heresy of the two sons, one divine, one human. Perhaps the only possible answer is that, without the divine Word, Jesus would be what some radical critics have argued for—someone whose outlook was entirely constructed from the ideas and expectations of the Old Testament!

D. M. Baillie develops the valid and useful analogy between the person of Christ and the paradox of the Christian's experience of grace—St. Paul's 'I, yet not I'. Critics of Chalcedon should remember that Christians hope to be by grace what Jesus is by right, 'partakers of the divine nature', and to have the Eternal Son directing, by his Spirit, our chaotic human nature. But it is not clear that Baillie is as successful as he thinks in attributing a human personality to Jesus. 'The only *anhypostasia* . . . is not a denial of personality, but a denial of independence'.[7] 'Complete dependance' would

---

4. W. Temple, *Christus Veritas*, Macmillan 1924, pp. 150, 151.
5. In contrast to the disastrous scholastic speculation that any of the three persons could, in principle, be incarnate; St. Thomas Aquinas, *Summa Theologica* III, iii, 5. No wonder the doctrine of the Trinity fell into disrepute.
6. W. Temple, *op. cit.* p. 150.
7. D. M. Baillie, *God was in Christ*, Faber 1948, p. 93.

properly describe the relation of the Son to the Father. It does not describe the relation of created human personality to God. The essence of creation is independence.[8]

'Perfect . . . without sin'. These two expressions from Chalcedon add an 'inhuman' tone to its definition. The New Testament never describes Jesus as perfect, though it does describe him as 'made perfect', 'perfected' (Hebrews 5:9). Jesus ascribes perfection to his Father (Matthew 5:48; Mark 10:18). 'Perfect in manhood' simply means 'fully, completely human'. But 'without sin' is a New Testament claim. Clearly it does not mean without temptation. Jesus was tempted, or tested, and found the experience agonizing. The line between temptation and sin is a fine one, and there are occasions when, humanly speaking, Jesus' reaction can seem less than perfect—to his mother, for example (John 2:4), to the Syrophoenician woman (Mark 7:27) and in the scathing denunciations of his opponents. But J. A. T. Robinson calls attention[9] to the lack of any consciousness of sin on Jesus' part (compared, for example, with St. Paul) and to the absence of any anxiety on the part of the gospel writers to defend him from such accusations as being 'a glutton and a drunkard, a friend of tax-collectors and sinners' (Matthew 11:19). In each event of the gospel story Jesus has wrestled with the dark side of human nature, his own and ours, and has emerged so victorious that the earlier stages of the conflict, where they are apparent to us, seem transfigured by the final victory. The Epistle to the Hebrews contains a summary which corresponds closely to the gospels and is one of the most profound descriptions of the human form divine:

8. According to R. V. Sellers, impersonal humanity 'means no more than that the manhood has no independent existence'. (*The Council of Chalcedon*, SPCK 1953, p. 345). Baillie's more acceptable alternative to *anhypostasia* is declared by Sellers to be its meaning! 'Person', says E. L. Mascall, 'is not . . . a constituent of human nature, it is a purely metaphysical term' (*Via Media*, Longmans 1956, p. 102); comparable, in other realms of discourse, to 'transcendental ego', or 'inmost being'.
9. *Op. cit.* pp. 97, 98.

In the days of his flesh he offered up prayers and supplications with loud cries and tears . . . Although he was a son he learned obedience through what he suffered, and being made perfect he became the source of eternal salvation to all who obey him.' (Hebrews 5:7–9).

CHAPTER TWELVE

Cross of the Father?

The doctrine of *impassibility* states that God is immune from suffering. The word comes from the same Latin root as *passion*, by which we describe the sufferings of Our Lord.

The history of the doctrine bears a general resemblance to that of the impersonal humanity of Christ. It was generally accepted by thinkers of all the main Christian traditions until about a century ago. In the last hundred years it has been vehemently denied, and much modern Christian discipleship would make the suffering of God an article of faith. As such it received perhaps its most famous expression in these much-quoted words from C. A. Dinsmore's *Atonement in Literature and Life* (1906):

> There was a cross in the heart of God before there was one planted on the green hill outside Jerusalem. And now that the cross of wood has been taken down, the one in the heart of God abides, and it will remain so long as there is one sinful soul for whom to suffer.[1]

The near universality of the doctrine of impassibility in

---

1. Quoted by J. K. Mozley, *The Impassibility of God*, Cambridge 1926, p. 148. Dinsmore made qualifications similar to those of Temple; see below.

earlier centuries is all the more surprising since the Bible, and in particular the Old Testament apparently teaches no such thing. It cheerfully attributes to God, not only human limbs and organs, but a range of human emotions. 'Love, joy, anger, jealousy, "repentance", are all ascribed to God, differing from the corresponding feelings in men only by their conformity with God's perfect righteousness'.[2] Nor does this apply only to 'primitive' parts of the Old Testament. Later Isaiah is very explicit:

> In all their afflictions he was afflicted . . .
> But they rebelled and grieved his holy Spirit
> (Isaiah 63:9, 10).

Early Christian theologians explained away such language as a mere concession to human ways of thinking. The God of the philosophers had effectively supplanted Jahweh. 'The divine nature is altogether separated from every affection of passion and change, and remains unmoved and unshaken for ever on that peak of blessedness.'[3]

Where the question of impassibility became fiercely controversial was in the doctrines of the Trinity and the Incarnation. Some theologians produced exaggerated forms of the 'Monarchian' approach to God which reduced almost to nothing the distinctions in the Godhead. Tertullian, brilliant at the memorable phrase, said of one of them, Praxeas, that he 'crucified the Father', meaning that Praxeas attributed the sufferings of Christ to the Father.[4] The name 'Patripassian' describes such a view. The widespread hatred of this doctrine, often called Sabellian, owes much to its ascription of suffering to God. When the question of the divine and human in Christ became prominent there was much dispute as to how and in what sense Christ suffered. One of the motives of the Antiochene School

2. J. K. Mozley, *op. cit.* p. 3.
3. Origen, *Homily on Numbers*, XXIII:2, quoted by J. K. Mozley, *op. cit.* p. 62.
4. Tertullian, *Adversus Praxean*, I.

in separating the natures in Christ was to preserve the impassibility of the divine. Some Alexandrian and Latin theologians minimised the reality of Christ's manhood, as we have seen, and minimised the reality of his sufferings at the same time.

Archbishop Temple drew attention to an important distinction.

> Aristotle's 'apathetic' God was enthroned in men's minds, and no idol has been found so hard to destroy. He reappears in the Greek fathers, and in the first of the Anglican Thirty-nine Articles. There is a highly technical sense in which God, as Christ revealed him, is 'without passions'; for he is Creator and supreme, and is never 'passive' in the sense of having things happen to him except with his consent . . . But the term really means 'incapable of suffering', and in this sense its predication of God is almost wholly false.[5]

Temple was cautious; his *almost* and a footnote explaining it, indicate that he is not as far from the main Christian tradition as the general impression of his words might suggest. God is, in fact, both passible and impassible; Temple's position is similar to that of Origen. Neither is able to resolve the paradox.

The Great War of 1914–1918 gave a powerful impetus to belief in a suffering God. The army chaplain G. A. Studdert Kennedy (1889–1929) made it his central message for men in the hopeless carnage of the trenches:

> The Universe was made as it is because it is the only way it could be made, and this way lays upon God the burden of many failures and of eternal strain—the sorrow of God the Father . . . God . . . is everywhere in history, but nowhere is he Almighty. Ever and always we see him suffering, striving, crucified but conquering.[6]

5. W. Temple, *Christus Veritas*, Macmillan 1924, p. 269.
6. *The Hardest Part*, 1918, quoted by J. K. Mozley, *op. cit.* p. 158.

> Father, if He, the Christ, were thy Revealer,
> 	Truly the First Begotten of the Lord,
> Then must thou be a Suff'rer and a Healer
> 	Pierced to the heart by the sorrow of the sword.[7]

The suffering of God has recently been restated in W. H. Vanstone's moving book *Love's Endeavour Love's Expense* (Darton, Longman and Todd 1977). This too arises from practical experience, not of war but of Christian ministry in the affluent society. It draws on human love and human creativity as analogies of God's relation to his creation.

> If God is love, and the universe is his creation, then for the being of the universe God is totally expended in precarious endeavour, of which the issue, as triumph or as tragedy, has passed from his hands. . . . He waits as the artist or the lover waits, having given all.

> Thou art God; no monarch thou
> 	Thron'd in easy state to reign;
> Thou art God, whose arms of love
> 	Aching, spent, the world sustain.[8]

Vanstone is undoubtedly looking in the right direction with his analogies. But one might wonder whether his glowing language does not lead him towards an identification of God with his creation which those analogies would not support. An artist is not merged into his work and a lover can survive unrequited love. Otherwise they would be unable to fulfil their roles— they would not be able to create or to be the giver and receiver of love.[9]

---

7. *The Suffering God*, quoted by A. Wilkinson, *The Church of England and the First World War*, SPCK 1978, p. 138.
8. *Op. cit.* p. 74 and p. 120.
9. 'The love of earthly lovers compels them at times to desire the abolition of all distinction even of the bare consciousness between each other . . . yet such abolition would abolish, at the same time, the joy of the mutual self-surrender and, indeed, everything therewith to love and which to love'—F. von Hügel, 'Suffering and God', in *Essays and Addresses on the Philosophy of Religion, Second Series*, Dent 1926, p. 195.

No-one pursued the analogy between God and the human creator more thoroughly and fruitfully than Dorothy L. Sayers, especially in *The Mind of the Maker* (Methuen 1941). Her approach led her to distinguish (in what is ultimately a trinitarian pattern) between the creative Idea and the creative Activity. The Idea is

> passionless, timeless, beholding the whole work complete at once, the end in the beginning: and this is the image of the Father.

The Activity is

> begotten of that idea, working in time from the beginning to the end, with sweat and passion, being incarnate in the bonds of matter; and this is the image of the Word.[10]

Sayers pursues the analogy between God and the literary creator in a variety of ways. For our present purpose her views on impassibility are particularly noteworthy:

> There are the Patripassians, who involve the Father—Idea in the vicissitudes and torments of the creative Activity. Patripassian authors are those who (in the common phrase) 'make it up as they go along'; serial writers are strongly tempted to this heresy. We might, I think, also class as Patripassian those works in which the Idea insensibly undergoes a change in the course of writing, so that the cumulative effect of the whole thing when read is something other than the effect to which all its parts are supposed to be working.[11]

If this analogy has anything to teach us, then we would not be serving the true interests of the love of

10. *Op. cit.* p. 28.
11. *Op. cit.* p. 141. The Sayers analogy shows a remarkable correspondence with expositions of impassibility like that of E. L. Mascall, where a 'totally suffering' God can neither initiate the human pilgrimage nor be its joyful goal (*Existence and Analogy*, Longmans 1949, Chapter 6).

God for his creation if we expounded that love in such a way as to put it totally at the mercy of the creation. It is as Word or Son that God creates, and as such he is 'totally expended'. It may be that Vanstone's theology is not necessarily opposed to this. What he sees as inimical, both to true love and to artistic creation, is what he calls the 'assured programme' which fails to take true account of the lover's and the creation's freedom. This is surely right, and can be given abundant human illustration. We have seen that the incarnate Son has an element of the questing and experimental about his sonship. The assured programme tends, in theology, to an inhuman Jesus and a doctrine of predestination. But the very word 'programme' relates, in the Sayers analogy, to the work of the Son; a flexible, waiting, agonized programme is consistent with, and indeed requires, an impassible Idea.

In any ordinary family analogy we would naturally think of a father sharing, at least in spirit, the sufferings of his son. But in most of the biblical analogies the human father or son suffers through some failure in their human relationship. Between God the Father and the Son there is no such failure. The Father acts through the Son, and the Son does the will of the Father, as in the parable of the Vineyard (Mark 12:1–12). There the father's feelings about the murder of his son are not in view. The point of the parable is the fate of the tenants, which, for good or ill, the father has always had within his purpose.

It is as Incarnate Son that God suffers. When the Epistle to the Hebrews denies that he has suffered 'repeatedly since the foundation of the world' (Hebrews 9:26) it is arguing for the uniqueness of the incarnation and its sacrifice, as compared with the repeated sacrifices of the temple. Suffering is a temporal process, closely linked with evil, and the incarnation is the point of God's involvement in it. Sympathy, but not suffering, is the proper description—necessarily analogical—for the Father's care of his creation. Baron von Hügel, bringing his massive spiritual insight to bear on the subject, denied that what human suffering most needs is a fellow sufferer.

Father Damien sympathized, he who had never
suffered leprosy, with the sufferings of the lepers
more, doubtless, than the average sufferer from
leprosy sympathized . . . How much more must
this be true of God, of Him who is omniscient?[12]

He also recognized that divine sympathy is something
'which we cannot succeed in picturing vividly without
drawing on our own experiences of ourselves, where
sympathy and suffering are so closely intertwined'.[13]
What we need is not patripassianism but a more
imaginative sense of participation in the sufferings of
the Son far beyond the boundaries of the visible church;
as though what he suffered once for all is shared out
and response to it made a means of salvation (Colossians 1:24).

12. *Art. cit.* p. 198.
13. *Art. cit.* p. 205.

CHAPTER THIRTEEN

Doctrine and Gender

Is God male? Scholars, answering rather testily, as though the question were unreasonable, usually say no.

> Theologians, mystics and seers have revolted against the idea that God is male.[1]
>
> I do not suggest, of course, that there is in the triune Godhead anything crudely corresponding to the biological characteristic of sex.[2]

One might be forgiven for thinking the opposite. 'Father', 'Son', and most of the other terms we use for God are masculine. 'Spirit' is not sexual, or necessarily human; the Greek *pneuma* is neuter gender. But the Bible's analogies for God are predominantly male. His main rival for human allegiance in Old Testament times was the earth mother, who 'begets' the visible world and shares with it an irrational mixture of kindness and ferocity. By contrast, Jahweh's relation with the world is defined by the analogy not of parenthood but of creation. He creates from will, not necessity, and is distinct from, but rationally related to, his creation. In primitive life where the male was the maker and the female the bearer of children the male analogy for God

1. V. A. Demant, 'Why the Christian priesthood is male', in *Women and Holy Orders*, CIO 1966, p. 101.
2. E. L. Mascall, 'Women and the Priesthood of the Church', in *Why Not?* Marcham Books 1972, p. 111.

was firmly and decisively chosen. For most of Christian history it has called for little comment and been taken for granted.

What has brought the question of gender in the deity to the fore is the women's liberation movement, and in particular—since it is the tangible and visible change which really rouses people—the ordination of women. Within the churches of the Anglican communion, where, at the time of writing, the controversy is most pronounced, conditions resemble somewhat the state of affairs just before the Council of Nicea (Chapter 9). Authority, especially authority favouring the change, urges those at odds to remain in, or return to, peace and fellowship, and sometimes grandly pronounces the matter to be of no great importance. But these exhortations will have no more effect than Constantine's. What is at issue is the doctrine of the image of God, and, moreover, the very practical expression of that doctrine in the face you see at the Lord's table. Controversies about God are very bitter. Students of church history are understandably appalled at the violence of the disputes about God and Christ in the fourth and fifth centuries, even when there was nothing visual to focus them. The early church is with us again in an unwelcome way.[3]

Feminism within the church often seeks to remove or diminish the male language about God. In the United States a prominent woman concelebrating the eucharist with the bishop at her ordination divided up the prayer of consecration so that she herself never addressed God as 'Father'—'We divided the Eucharistic prayer so that each of us spoke separately, and I stuck him with all the

---

3. 'By 1965 eleven women had been ordained to the priesthood (in Sweden); and the Church of Sweden has lost a far higher number of men ordinands who withdrew from ordination, and clergymen who laid down the practice of their ministry, because of the ordination of women. There is no evidence that the controversy has lost any of its bitterness, or is within sight of an end'—*Women and Holy Orders*, p. 21. Female ordination in the Episcopal church of America has produced schism and bitterness, and there has been a large decline in church membership. See R. E. Terwilliger, 'A Fractured Church', in *Man, Woman and Priesthood*, SPCK 1978.

''Fathers''.'[4] On the other hand, some feminists have concluded that Christianity is hopelessly and irrevocably committed to male language about God. 'Many a feminist and conservative Christian join hands in agreeing that Christianity is essentially tied to a symbol system in which God is conceived as male. The implication for such a feminist is that this cannot be her religion.'[5]

'Tied to a symbol system in which God is conceived as male'—this, if cumbrous to avoid saying too little or too much, is no more than the truth. As Karl Barth might say, God has conferred on the human male certain attributes which reflect his own perfect maleness, notably creativity, and finding love and response in the female, who in consequence receives the attribute of mankind and creation responding to God.

Such analogical language is at once authoritative and opaque. If we dismiss it, we dismiss, by implication, God's revelation. But we are left to work out the force and limits of the analogy. We do not know, by reason or intuition, what perfect maleness or femaleness is; we may expect, in the life of the faith, to be shown it, and then to be able to speak of it.

But have we not, in a special sense, been shown it? At the incarnation the eternal Son took flesh in the womb of the blessed virgin Mary. The Father (if Tertullian was right) acted as Father in bringing about the conception of his Son, but 'by the Holy Spirit' and without the physical copulation which pagan gods organized for themselves. How like, yet how unlike, human paternity! By this operation both maleness and femaleness are made flesh. St. Mary stands for, and leads, the whole of humanity and creation in loving response to God. This, the divinely-appointed female role, is powerfully stated by St. John.

> And a great portent appeared in heaven, a woman clothed with the sun, with the moon under her

4. W. Oddie, *What will happen to God?* SPCK 1984, p. 105.
5. Daphne Hampson, 'The Challenge of Feminism to Christianity', in *Theology* September 1985, p. 345.

feet, and on her head a crown of twelve stars . . .
And the dragon stood before the woman who was
about to bear a child, that he might devour her
child when he brought it forth; she brought forth a
male child, one who was to rule all nations with a
rod of iron, but her child was caught up to God and
his throne, and the woman fled into the wilderness,
where she has a place prepared by God.

(Revelation 12:1, 4–6)

A male child: the Eternal Son took male human
nature in the virgin's womb, so uniting it with God for
ever, taking it through life and death to the throne of
God, so that 'God, the flesh of God, hath reigned'.[6]
Christian orthodoxy requires us to hold that, from the
incarnation and to all eternity, God has a male human
body; and this must correspond to God's intention *from*
all eternity.

There are, at the beginning of Genesis, two accounts
of the creation of mankind, one as the work of the sixth
day in the Seven Days of Creation (Genesis 1:1–2:4a)
and the other at the beginning of the Garden of Eden
story (Genesis 2:4b—end). The distinction between
these two accounts, only the second of which uses the
divine name Jahweh, is one of the foundations of the
critical study of the Old Testament. But as Jewish and
Christian scripture they must be assumed to teach a
common truth, however wrong it may be to try to
harmonize them as literature.

In Genesis 1 God creates man, male and female, 'in
his own image' as the climax of his works. In Genesis 2
nothing is said about the image, and God created the
male before the animals. Then, finding 'no helper fit for
him', he creates the woman from his rib.

It is commonly thought that Genesis 1 teaches the
equality of the sexes and Genesis 2 the superiority of the
male. In schemes of progressive revelation the second,
as the earlier and more 'primitive', could be discounted.
But such cavalier treatment is not open to those who

---

6. *Regnat Deus, Dei caro,* from the Ascensiontide hymn *Aeterne Rex,*
   English Hymnal 141.

take the Bible seriously. M. E. Thrall attempted[7] to do justice to both accounts by making the first the ideal to be achieved and the second the actual or temporary situation; but this in practice is little more than a refinement of the 'progressive revelation' approach. Let us put it rather differently.

By creating mankind, male and female, in his own image, God declares his intention to take humanity to himself to save it, male and female. This salvation is conferred by our common baptism. 'For as many of you as were baptized into Christ have put on Christ. There is neither Jew nor Greek, there is neither slave nor free, there is neither male nor female' (Galatians 3:27, 28). The Eden story shows that it is male human nature God will take for his own flesh and female nature which will be creation's response; a distinction expressed in ordination and the male headship of marriage. 'The husband is the head of the wife as Christ is the head of the church, his body, and is himself its saviour' (Ephesians 5:23). Daphne Hampson says Christ's male humanity excludes women from salvation, for 'what God did not take on he did not redeem'.[8] But God has 'taken on' both male and female nature, though in different ways.[9]

If Daphne Hampson is right that Christianity cannot lose its male language about God and still be Christianity, she is utterly wrong in her deduction that Christianity is no religion for women. She is wrong both in theory and in practice. In Christianity, she says, 'women cannot . . . identify with the symbol of their God'.[10] But we do

7. *The Ordination of Women to the Priesthood*, SCM 1958.
8. *Art. cit.* p. 344. The phrase is based on Gregory of Nazianzus' criticism of Apollinarius in the late fourth century. Apollinarius developed a view of the incarnation in which the Son had no human mind—the *Logos* took 'flesh' in the sense of a material body. Gregory said, 'What is not *assumed* is not redeemed'.
9. Attempts to find a 'feminine principle' in the deity are unsuccessful and unnecessary. Sometimes they stem from a view that fatherhood alone is too stern; but in the Old Testament it can be very tender. See, e.g. I Samuel 18:33 and Hosea 11:1–4. Julian of Norwich's 'confusing but splendid' imagery is not a basis for doctrine. See Demant, *art. cit.* pp. 101–2.
10. *Art. cit.* pp. 344–5.

not live by 'identifying', we live (like the persons of the Trinity) by 'relating', or by a balance of the two. Marriage, and every human relationship, to some degree, depends on the *distinction* of the partners. If they are too alike, it will not work. They need to complement each other in a relationship of *polarity*. Men and women will relate to a 'male' God in subtly different ways. But there is no hint or suggestion that men who 'identify' with God, or Christ, do better than women who 'relate'. In human affairs we have not only the unique and dominating relationship of marriage, where 'identifying' is not the key concept; there is also the strength of mother—son and father—daughter relationships. Indeed, since the female is the sign for relating or responding to God, one might expect males to complain that, as believers and disciples, they are cast in a role which is natural for women but not for them, and so are at a disadvantage.

And in practice, is it not common knowledge that women vastly outnumber men in the pews of our churches? For whatever variety of reasons, women find it easier to relate to God. The whole life of the church bears this out. The Mothers' Union goes from strength to strength, and no other church organisation can compare with it. The Church of England Men's Society has died out. Anglicanism has many more nuns than monks, and mixed choirs have a strong tendency to go female.[11] Some years ago, before the present movement for the ordination of women, an unconventional parish priest related the preponderance of women, half facetiously, to the male ministry. If you want men to come to church, he said, you must ordain women. The deduction is invalid because of the ambiguous position of the female priest, but he saw the point of polarity or relatedness.

One way or another, within the institutional church or out of it, feminism seeks to change the image of God.

---

11. The point seems true not only in our individualistic and pietistic culture, but in areas of 'tribal' Christianity like Ireland and Greece, where the women go to church and the men stand around outside talking and smoking.

What to? Not, presumably, to the mother or the female; that would merely reproduce, in feminine terms, the disadvantages feminism alleges in the masculine terms. But all the humanity we know is either male or female. So the logic of the feminist scheme is that there is no human image of God. Destroy the image and you destroy belief. There are more effective ways to atheism than the overt and aggressive denial of God's existence. Make God remote, unknowable, unimaginable, and put a gulf between him and Jesus, and you will do the devil's work without knowing it. It is what Arius did; and those theologians and church leaders today who are busy dissolving or diluting Christian doctrine will be found in favour of the ordination of women.

CHAPTER FOURTEEN

Daughters of Aaron?

Arguments for the ordination of women draw their force from secular movements and changes. They try not to, but the disclaimer is not convincing. Of course if ordination is solely a matter of reflecting social convention there is no reason why it should not reflect the social convention of the present.

Even so, the attempt to discover progress in the position of women from subordination to equality is mistaken. 'The denigration of women is not an age-long habit which has lately been cured by historical advance.'[1] It is arguable that the opening-up of certain male institutions and professions to women has not benefited women in general and has made little difference to society as a whole. Nevertheless the tendency to see the priesthood as one of the last bastions to be captured is strong, and the inability of women to fulfil what they consider to be a vocation to ordination appears as a denial of right and equality. Opposition to the ordination of women takes a number of forms. The practical difficulty, in relation to marriage and the family, is less weighty than formerly, now that it is seen to be *possible* for women to undertake roles previously male. There are arguments from tradition (a male priesthood in the Bible and the church), from ecumenism (relations with

---

1. V. A. Demant, 'Why the Christian Priesthood is male', in *Women and Holy Orders*, CIO 1966, p. 104.

the Roman Catholic and Orthodox churches) and from the supposed psychological differences between men and women. These points have often been discussed and they do not fall within the scope of this study.

The argument from the being and revelation of God is not easy to state, and is apt to sound abstruse or to prove too much. When V. A. Demant, in an otherwise clear and trenchant article, says, 'The Christian revelation, as a Logos-centred salvation religion, naturally requires a male priesthood',[2] his claim is neither obvious nor overwhelming. The maleness of the priesthood stands or falls by its relation to the Father and the Son.

We have argued that there is, in Christianity, both a universal salvation by baptism and a restricted ordination. The gender sign of the first is female (though it includes both men and women). The gender sign of the second is male; and since it is selective, not for its own sake but for God and the church, it is *actually* male. A mixed ordination confuses the gender signs and no longer relates to the different ways God has taken male and female human nature to himself.[3]

There are no real analogies from secular affairs. The admission of women to Parliament and various professions is relevant only if the economy of the church is a matter for human arrangement. The possibility, in the British Constitution, of a female sovereign might be thought to have some bearing on the subject, for the Christian monarch is an anointed and consecrated person who is, in some sense, a representative of God. The term 'Vicar (=deputy) of Christ' was first used of monarchs.

Many monarchical traditions (following the 'Salic'

---

2. *Art. cit.* p. 102.
3. Without being consciously derived from it, this differentiation corresponds to C. G. Jung's two 'intuitive concepts', *Logos* and *Eros*. 'The *Logos* is that which discriminates, differentiates, and brings order out of chaos; *Eros* is a principle of relatedness, connection and receptivity . . . the *Logos* function is characteristic of the masculine consciousness, and *Eros* of the feminine consciousness.'—R. F. Hobson, 'Psychological Considerations' in *Women and Holy Orders*, CIO 1960, p. 58.

law) do not recognize female succession. In those which do it operates only in an absence of brothers.[4] All reigning queens in Britain have found their position very difficult, and all except one leant heavily on male support. The exception, Queen Elizabeth I, performed her role only at great cost to her own personality. Monarchy, in contrast to ordination, is not a specifically Christian institution, though capable of Christian consecration. It would be hazardous to draw any encouragement for women's ordination from something comparable only in a very limited degree.

In the 'catholic' tradition the controversy over the ordination of women focuses on the presidency of the eucharist, the characteristic role of the ordained. An attempt has recently been made[5] by the Bishop of Salisbury (J. A. Baker) to show that a 'catholic' or 'high' view of the eucharist is consistent with the ordination of women and may even encourage it. 'Christ and his sacrifice', he says, 'are contained and communicated within the consecrated elements', and consecration could be effected by any 'officially appointed representative of the church'.[6] The idea that the celebrating priest is an image or icon of Christ the Son is regarded by the Bishop as obscuring the truth of the real presence of Christ in the elements, and the distancing of Christ from the celebrant by varying the latter's gender seems to him desirable.

From the Reformation there has commonly been a gulf between those who located Christ in the bread and wine and those who located him in the faithful worshipper. Modern thought, including the Anglican-Roman Catholic International Commission[7] is strongly

4. Recently Sweden changed its law to give the right of the royal succession to the eldest child, male or female; a logical change, after the ordination of women. Modern Sweden cannot be said to value either its monarchy or its priesthood very highly.
5. J. A. Baker, 'Eucharistic Presidency and Women's Ordination', in *Theology*, September 1985.
6. *Art. cit.* p. 357 and p. 354.
7. Anglican-Roman Catholic International Commission, *The Final Report*, CTS/SPCK 1982, 'Eucharistic Doctrine—The Statement' III.7 (p. 15) and 'Elucidation' 7 (p. 22).

inclined to see these approaches as complementary rather than contradictory. It is extraordinary that the Bishop should invoke a 'consecration by formula' doctrine as the whole eucharistic mystery, ignoring the character of the participants and the relation of the body of worshippers at each service to its earthly head and leader.

He considers also whether the eucharist is, or is not, a re-enactment of the Last Supper, deciding, quite rightly, that the remembrance of which it speaks is a remembrance not of the Supper but of the Lord's death and resurrection in a form supplied by the Supper. How this affects the gender of the celebrant is not clear. There is no call to reproduce the exact table arrangements of the Last Supper, even if we knew what they were. But the invisible celebrant is still Christ the Son, eternally offering love and praise to the Father. If a male priest is the appropriate representative of the Christ of the Last Supper, he is the appropriate representative also of the Christ at the right hand of the Father.[8]

As is often pointed out, celebrating the eucharist requires none of the accomplishments needed for the various activities of the teaching and pastoral ministry. It is highly appropriate that it should be the characteristic act of the ordained, because it makes the point that the basis of ordination is not merit. An element of merit enters the process of individual selection, but it remains true that 'the unworthiness of ministers hindereth not the effect of the sacrament'.[9] Like God's common salvation by baptism, his choice of the male sex for ordination is by grace and not by merit. At the eucharist, the male presbyter and the 'spouse and body of Christ'[10] relate to each other in and through the sacrament as the visual, local, earthly expression of God's salvation.

As God's decree, ordination is both a privilege and a burden. Because of it, a layman is always a second ranker in the church. A laywoman has, within her own

8. Dorothy L. Sayers called the female priest 'Sarah Bernhardt playing Hamlet'; quoted by V. A. Demant, *art. cit.* p. 113.
9. Article XXVI of the XXXIX Articles of the Church of England.
10. Ordering of Priests, *Book of Common Prayer*.

sex, no such inferiority. She can discover and exercise her ministry[11] without any 'order' of women to make it inherently second class. Much is said about the frustration of women wishing to be ordained. It is pertinent also to consider that much larger, but less articulate body of women for whom women's ordination would be demotion—the nuns and sisters, the parsons' wives, the countless and varied ministers of tea and sympathy, of broom and flower and laundry—those on whom the life of the church depends, and who give reality and substance to its corporate *persona* as female.[12]

We should expect that ordination, which is a privilege, should also prove a burden. It creates anticlericalism—much more a male than a female phenomenon, ranging from the anticlericalism of murder and revolution in the Latin tradition to the Anglo-Saxon anticlericalism of giggle and embarrassment. In defence of anticlericals it must be said that ordination can have a deplorable effect on character, making clerics bossy, devious and untruthful. The expectation that women's ordination would remove these blemishes is a forlorn one. Some advocates give expression to the hope that women will do it better—a fatal self-righteousness, and recognized as such both by human experience and the fierce condemnation of Our Lord (Matthew 23:30, 31).

There remains the view that a male priesthood is 'maimed' and 'lacks the services of half the human race'. This frank appeal to worldliness and reduction of ordination to the status of a lay profession recalls *The Great Divorce*, by C. S. Lewis,[13] where the damned

11. Ordination is not the same as ministry. Clergymen minister, but so do all active Christians. Many women have a great gift for uninstitutionalized ministry. Some parsons' wives are better at it than their husbands; their ministry depends on the fact that he is ordained and *she is not*.

12. Describing women's ministry Evelyn Underhill wrote, 'The question of status, scope and so forth has never . . . entered their minds at all. We notice in them a sort of beautiful informality and freedom in their proceedings; and something which we might call a maternal and domestic quality in their method'—*Mixed Pasture*, Methuen 1933, quoted by V. A. Demant, *art. cit.* pp. 113–114.

13. Bles 1946, p. 43.

bishop thought Our Lord would have been much more effective if he had lived to maturity and not thrown his life away on the cross. It is a short step to saying he cannot be an adequate saviour of the world, for he was male, and unmarried.[14, 15]

14. At the time of writing the Church of England is proposing to ordain women as deacons but not as priests or bishops; a compromise acceptable to some conservatives because deacons do not celebrate the eucharist. This move to 'divide the substance' of holy order is doomed to failure. It is ordination, even more than the distinctions within orders, which is the divine ordinance; and women, admitted to the first but not subsequent grades, will have *for the first time* the legitimate grievance that they are kept in an inferior position.

15. These chapters were written before the publication of Mary Hayter's *The New Eve in Christ*, SPCK 1987. Subtitled 'The Use and Abuse of the Bible in the Debate about Women in the Church', this book argues that the ordination of women is consistent with 'mainstream' understanding of the Bible and the Christian revelation. But in spite of some good insights the cost is high. Male language about God is devalued and the image of God is blurred. Dr. Hayter observes, quite rightly, that the Old Testament is sparing in calling God 'Father', but she wrongly ascribes this to limitation of the male image of God, whereas it is *paternity in relation to mankind* from which God is distanced. The male priesthood of the old covenant, the male human nature of Christ and the maleness of the apostolate are all dismissed as 'culturally conditioned'. The heavy reliance on the views of G. W. H. Lampe confirms the point made at the end of Chapter 13—the ordination of women undermines the doctrines of the Trinity and the Incarnation.

CHAPTER FIFTEEN

Doctrine and Deviation

The scientific study of the human personality or *psyche*, psychology, is more recent than biblical criticism, but has produced, in its own area, a comparable change in our thinking. We now have words and definitions for things previously known only by intuition. The forces of the mind have been *named*, by Freud and his successors, and modern man has a degree of self-consciousness about them like the 'knowledge of good and evil' which came to Adam. We know that men and women have different degrees of masculinity and femininity. We know that, in contrast to the predominant and 'normal' pattern, some are attracted exclusively to members of their own sex, and are consequently called *homosexual*—the adjectival prefix *homo* (the same) is the one used in the doctrinal term *homoousios* (Chapter 9). A larger number, while conforming to the marital pattern, are capable of acting homosexually under certain circumstances, and are called *bisexual*.

The evaluation of sexual deviancy, both the condition and the activity, has been prominent lately in the church and in the world. In England the law was changed in 1967 to make acts between consenting adult males in private no longer illegal (similar acts between females never were illegal). This has resulted in a much greater public awareness of sexual deviation, with greater expression of it in literature, art and advertisement.

Although homosexuality is a female, as well as a male, phenomenon, 'lesbianism'[1] is so far less evident and less organized than its male counterpart. Lesbians are often strong in the feminist movement and feel that their handicap is not lesbianism but womanhood. Male homosexuality, on the other hand, itself constitutes a pressure group in society similar to feminism, demanding equality and liberation, and giving voice to the slogans of the self-righteous and self-pitying minority.

Male and female, however, are never neatly parallel. Feminism has seen as its goal the entry into male preserves, including Christian ordination. Homosexuals, on the other hand, look for social acceptability for themselves and their relationships. This means, in particular, the recognition by church and state of homosexual marriages. It is significant that the American Episcopal church which approved the ordination of women was faced a year later with the demand for homosexual marriage. This they did not accede to.

Marriage 'means Christ and the church' (Ephesians 5:32), and these two, as we have seen, bear the gender signs of male and female. Marriage must therefore be between male and female and not between two persons of the same sex. Homosexuals are still men and women. An effeminate man is still a man, and a masculine woman is still a woman—not only in some philosophical sense, but biologically and psychologically. Hermaphrodites, who have the physical attributes of both sexes, are rare and quite another matter.

We must, in the celebration of the church's sacraments, maintain the integrity of the gender signs. Not to do so would make us deviationists in doctrine, or heretics, as earlier and harsher ages would say.[2] But this will not, of itself, alter the psychology of individual men and women. Western man, under the influence of Christianity, has increased in individuality, and the range of personality within both male and female is more open and self-conscious. The psychologists have

1. So called after the Aegean island of Lesbos, the home of Sappho who, in the sixth century BC wrote passionate poems about her women friends.
2. Sexual deviation is to the modern world what doctrinal heresy and ecclesiastical dissent were in the past. Society has not become more tolerant, but the pressure to conform has shifted to different areas of life.

named our variety; and what has once been named cannot revert to its earlier and unselfconscious state.

The point is made, in particular, in a controversy which arose out of the report *Homosexual Relationships* (CIO 1979). A working party was appointed by the Board for Social Responsibility of the General Synod of the Church of England to study homosexuality. In the course of its report, which included biblical, theological, medical and legal evidence, the working party concluded that the *concept* of homosexuality was unknown to the ancient world in general and to the biblical writers in particular. What they meant was that homosexual acts were familiar and perhaps widespread, but they were not performed by persons *incapable* of normal intercourse. The homosexual condition, they thought, is a product of modern society and one for which the Bible does not directly legislate.

The Board, in publishing the report, was unhappy with this view, which might lead to some degree of permissiveness in relation to homosexual activity. Accordingly it appended some 'critical observations' which suggested that it regretted setting up a working party—or this particular working party at any rate. It countered the report's view of the homosexual condition by quoting some evidence from the Bible and church history. Since, however, this evidence concerned celibacy and impotence it is difficult to see its relevance. In the ascetic ages of the church celibacy was certainly not synonymous with homosexuality, and impotence could have various causes. Many of the biblical condemnations of homosexual acts are in the setting of rape and prostitution, which again have no necessary connection with the homosexual condition. St. Paul's 'sin list' in I Corinthians 6:9, 10 includes certain deviant acts, but the use of the word 'homosexuals' to denote what is condemned, implying the person or the condition rather than the activity, is a surprising mistranslation by the Revised Standard version of 1952. So in this particular controversy the honours so far would seem to go to the working party rather than to its parent body.

The most famous reference to the subject in the Bible, and the one which gives us the word 'sodomy', is the story of Sodom and Gomorrah in Genesis 19. It has been questioned whether this originally implied sexual activity at all; the verb 'to know' is ambiguous, perhaps deliberately so. But if the traditional interpretation is correct, the story is about the inhospitable attempted rape of the angel of Jahweh, for which outrage the subsequent fire and brimstone is a fitting retribution. It is a long way from 'consenting adults in private'.[3]

St. Paul's treatment of homosexuality at the beginning of the Epistle to the Romans is commonly regarded as evidence of his anti-deviationism (just as I Corinthians 7 is often represented as being 'against women'). It is, however, significant that he regards homosexual activity as itself a *punishment*—a corporate punishment—for radical doctrinal error. Because men did not recognize the true God but worshipped images (Romans 1:18–23) he *gave them up* (vv. 24, 26) to dishonourable passions. In the case of both men and women St. Paul implies that they could, and did, have normal relations as well. We should perhaps imagine St. Paul surveying the sexual licence of the Greek and Roman world, and making a connection with the gods they worshipped—a reasonable enough connection, since the gods did these things themselves.

The Pauline insight, that sexual deviation is a punishment visited on society as a whole, finds a modern psychological parallel. Though there is no consensus about the precise origin of sexual deviation, there is wide agreement that it reflects a child's very early experiences and relationship with its family. An imbalance (which may, in turn, be no-one's individual fault) can result in deviation. So 'the sins of the fathers are visited on the children' (Exodus 20:5) whatever indignant individualists say. We are bound together and we affect one another.

Our Christian duty is to maintain the doctrinal gender signs. We must not alter the maleness of God's image or of the priesthood, nor compromise marriage as the relation of male and female. To do so would be to

3. The Church of England's daily lectionary for Morning and Evening Prayer omits the vital verses of Genesis 19—a pointless piece of prudery.

betray God's revelation and do no service to the human race whose health and salvation depend on it. But the revelation has, directly or indirectly, changed us, and we must take account of the change. An ethic, sexual or not, must involve both fulfilment and self-denial. Can we relate this to homosexuals?

One misfortune of the decline of asceticism and the monastic life is that our society is too dominated by marriage. That may seem a strange thing to say in a situation of widespread illegitimacy and marriage breakdown. But these things themselves, the 'living together' and frequent remarriage, testify to the enormous power of the idea of marriage, however imperfectly achieved, and there is no other comparable image or ideal for those not meant for marriage. So, for homosexuals, fulfilment can come only by a homosexual marriage. Such young men looking for a partner exhibit the entire range of attitudes of a girl identifying her husband; only to be disillusioned and shattered sooner or later—usually sooner. This is a form of brain-washing by society. Homosexuals should look, and the church should help them look, for another image of fulfilment. Marriage is not for them. In this way they must deny themselves, as Our Lord did.

But it may be that other relationships could provide a positive image and a degree of fulfilment. Much of this book has been about fathers and sons. It is a common experience that male homosexuality is associated with some inadequacy in the father—son relationship, such as the absence of a father, or an unduly mild father. (The absence of a father has a serious, but not usually *sexual*, effect on daughters.) Life then becomes the search for a father. It does not seem that the fatherhood of God is meant to be a *substitute* for human fatherhood. When Jahweh said of Adam, 'It is not good for the man to be alone' (Genesis 2:18), he never suggested that fellowship with his creator was the answer to *this* need, and those who have no Eve to cleave to might look to have a 'foster father'. Perhaps the figure of St. Joseph has a continuing role to play in the life of humanity.

With some homosexuals it is the other way round. Deprived of, or unsatisfied by, physical fatherhood, their search is for the son who has eluded them. Happy are those where (as in all human relationships) need and gift can be matched.

The father—son relationship might provide an image within which homosexuals could obtain company and fulfilment. Each contributes to the relationship what is characteristic of his age and outlook; a generation gap (maybe) is there to require of each a degree of self-denial, as families know so well. No particular permanence is vowed, on the analogy of the son who may leave home. Responsibility, not exclusiveness, is the mark of the relationship.

In some cases the appropriate image is not that of father and son, but of two sons engaged in a joint venture, as was suggested in Chapter 7. The Freudian tradition would regard this as widespread and natural for adolescents, but pathological when prolonged into maturity. But Freudianism is moralism with God left out. With the pluralism of personality in our society the 'two sons' image may be a proper one for some people for most, or all, of their lives.

But, whatever the image of the relationship, what about explicitly sexual, that is, genital, activity? The Church of England Working Party clearly agonized over this, torn between the traditional view that all homosexual acts were wrong and the homosexual demand for equality and freedom of physical expression. They did not endorse either view, but while re-affirming the normality and centrality of marriage concluded that the 'physical expression of sexual love' between homosexuals was not unthinkable. This sympathy with the deviant predicament combined with a broadly 'orthodox' approach found generous expression in the American Hale lectures of 1932, given by the priest-doctor J. R. Oliver, and published as *Psychiatry and Mental Health* (Scribner 1933). Advising counsellors of the homosexual, Oliver said, 'Show him how he can make his particular type of love as ideal and as fine as the love of Jonathan for David. Give him continence as an ideal. But tell him not to despair if he cannot always live up to it.'[4]

4. *Op. cit.* p. 255.

Part of our difficulty is that the ideal of continence is weak in our society, and that is primarily the fault of the normal majority, whose insistence on copulation on demand (without risk of conception) arouses deviants to expect the same. The idea that every human being must have a certain amount of genital activity is culturally conditioned, and until we have altered the cultural conditioning we shall continue to have the Working Party's dilemma. Weaning homosexuals away from the 'marriage' image would be a step in the right direction.

The biblical tradition sees nothing strange in physical affection between members of the same sex. The relation of David and Jonathan has already been referred to, and the one example of physical affection recorded of the incarnate Son is with the disciple whom he loved (John 13:23)—an incident which the appendix to the gospel goes out of its way to refer to (John 21:20).

Marriage is made in the image of Christ and the church, and intercourse and procreation are inherent in it. Homosexual relationships are made in the image of the Father and the Son; intercourse is not inherent in them and procreation is impossible. One of the few generalizations it seems safe to make about homosexual relations is that the more they are concerned with things other than 'sex' the more fruitful they are likely to be. Emancipation, which enables or encourages concentration on genital activity, is a dubious blessing and a double-edged achievement. Physical and mental illness may produce a reaction, in the spirit of John Keble's prayer, 'Save, Lord, by love or fear.'[5] It is the church's work and duty to look into its treasury to see what love and help it can give to both the majority and to minorities in this world which the church has, very largely, created, so that they may 'grow up in every way' 'until we all attain to the unity of the faith and of the knowledge of the Son of God, to mature manhood, to the measure of the stature of the fulness of Christ' (Ephesians 4:15, 13).

5. J. Keble, 'Whitsunday', in *The Christian Year*, 1827. The Acquired Immune Deficiency Syndrome (AIDS), like all such disasters, is a judgement on society, rather than on individuals.

Indexes

Index of Subjects and Places

Index of Extra-Biblical Names
and Writings

Some Reviews of
A DETECTION OF THE TRINITY
by John Thurmer

"This is a short but weighty and well-annotated study of the central doctrine of our Faith. . . . This is a book well worth reading—a multum in parvo."

The English Churchman

"As a commendation of the theology of Dorothy Sayers, this essay is appropriately whimsical. But it is well-informed and, at its serious heart, persuasive."

The Church Times

"This book is an imaginative attempt to make the doctrine of the Trinity intelligible and preachable by non-specialist clergy to equally non-specialist congregations. As such it meets a real need at a time when Christian doctrine is being challenged and often repudiated by theologians. . . . For those who scrape around on Trinity Sunday, looking for something to say, this would be a good place to begin."

Gerald Bray, *The Churchman*

"A most useful book concerning the Trinity, and one which is both academic and devotional."

Baptist Times

"An ideal medium for stimulating one's thoughts on the nature of the Triune God."

The Officer

"The book examines with great care the words we use, and which others have used in describing God, and the human experiences which give meaning to the words. Dorothy Sayers in her book, 'The Mind of the Maker' analysed the action of creation into Idea, Activity and Power, and related these to the three Persons of the Holy Trinity. By using her insights and other analogies, this author makes the doctrine of the Trinity accessible to us on the basis of our own human experience, and the ways in which we interpret it."

Kenneth G. Greet in *Faith and Thought*